ENTREPRENEUR WEALTH MANAGEMENT MADE EASY

Entrepreneur
Wealth
Management
Made Easy

BUILDING WEALTH BEYOND BUSINESS
AND LIFE BEYOND WORK

MICHAEL ZHUANG

LIONCREST
PUBLISHING

ENTREPRENEUR WEALTH MANAGEMENT MADE EASY
Ensuring Wealth Beyond Business and Life Beyond Work

ISBN   978-1-5445-0307-3   *Paperback*
       978-1-5445-0306-6   *Ebook*

Contents

Introduction

I met Damocles about ten years ago. He was a vigorous seventy at the time, and I happened to be seated next to him at a venture capital conference held in a downtown high-rise.

Maybe you've been to one of these conferences, where established businesspeople with money to invest—mostly older men—come to mix with eager young people pitching nifty ideas.

I'd accepted the invitation more out of curiosity than a desire to jump into a new business, but I sat with the group of potential investors. Before the show started, I started exchanging pleasantries with this remarkable man.

I was immediately impressed. Damocles had built up a line of minicomputers back in the 1980s and then successfully sold his business to IBM when he was in his fifties, just before minicomputers became obsolete. IBM had paid him tens of millions of dollars, equivalent to much more in today's money.

He'd been retired for nearly two decades, and he had that wonderful look—the relaxed smile of a wealthy, accomplished man. I learned that he lived in a fabulous neighborhood, right next to the Congressional Country Club. He and I enjoyed the show together, laughing at the questionable pitches and comparing notes on the best ideas.

We exchanged cards, and a few days later, I gave my new friend a call. I'm on the board of a nonprofit that provides social support to kids with cancer and their families. Our annual gala was coming up, and I was expected to invite as many wealthy people as I could—folks who could afford the $250-a-plate ticket. Because he lived nearby, Damocles seemed like a sure bet.

When I called, we again chatted agreeably, but when I asked if he'd attend the gala, he hesitated. I began to explain how meaningful I found the work of this nonprofit, but he didn't let me go on too long before he interrupted.

"Michael, it's not that I don't want to help. It's that I don't have the money."

I laughed because I honestly thought he was joking. "No way! Didn't you make tens of millions of dollars when you sold your company?"

"Yes," said Damocles, "but I've made a few financial mistakes since I retired. You might call them big mistakes. I'm now down to my last $200,000."

I still thought he was kidding. "Come on! Just the other day, we met at a venture capital event. Weren't you there looking for new ideas to invest in?"

"No, Michael. I wasn't there looking to invest. I was looking for a job. I'm pretty desperate, and I thought maybe one of these startups needed a CEO. That's the only job I know how to do—be a great CEO. Unfortunately, nobody wants a seventy-year-old CEO."

Damocles is not my friend's real name, of course, and I won't burden you with all the mistakes he made with his money over the years. I will only mention the dot-com bubble at the turn of the new century and the fact that Damocles had a stockbroker for a son.

THE SWORD ABOVE THE THRONE

In the ancient Greek tale, Damocles lived in the court of Dionysius II of Syracuse. One day, when he was praising the power and wealth of Dionysius, extolling the king's great fortune and magnificence, Dionysius made Damocles an offer. The king suggested that his courtier switch places with him for one day so Damocles could really understand what it felt like to be so fortunate and magnificent.

Naturally, Damocles accepted. The next day, he seated himself eagerly on the king's throne, surrounded by gold and silver and attendants. But to ensure that Damocles got a full understanding of a great fortune, Dionysius arranged that a gigantic sword be hung right above the throne, suspended by a single hair from a horse's tail.

All day long, Damocles stared nervously up at that sword, until he finally begged the king to release him from the throne, realizing that with great fortune and power always comes great danger.

When he related this tale, the philosopher Cicero asked, "Does not Dionysius seem to have made it sufficiently clear that there can be nothing happy for the person over whom some fear always looms?"

As a financial advisor who works with many wealthy individuals, the conversation with my own Damocles really shook me. I asked myself, "How could a person so successful in business—a former CEO—make so many mistakes and do such bad planning with their own money?"

I began to think about the successful entrepreneurs I knew in my advisory and quickly realized that the mistakes of this particular Damocles were not at all unusual. When I did a little research, I found his situation quite common.

In fact, I found examples right in my own family.

I have a group of relatives who were natural entrepreneurs. For a time, they were extremely wealthy and were the envy of everyone I knew when I was growing up. These relatives started in the garment industry back in China and then moved into large-scale recycling when they came to the United States. They figured out how to collect massive quantities of copper wiring and electrical components—even whole ships—and send them over to China for separation and processing.

As their wealth expanded, so did their businesses. They moved into power generation in China. Then tourism to China. Unlike most people, they not only saw brilliant opportunities but also made the most of those opportunities and had the much-celebrated entrepreneurial courage to take risks. Eventually, they worked out of an office in a Manhattan skyscraper, threw enormous parties, and bought spectacular homes.

But all along, these very smart people failed to notice the sword hanging above their heads. It was a sword that hung by a single thread: the trade policies of the Chinese governing imports, tourism, and joint ventures. When one day, lo and behold, government officials made changes to these policies, all the family enterprises came tumbling down in the space of just two years.

To the shock of my extended clan, these once-awesome relatives went bankrupt.

When that occurred, the great patriarch of the businesses was in his eighties, and he lived to see all three of his sons go bankrupt with him. One son even went to jail. Can you imagine falling from that height when you are in your eighties? Can you imagine seeing your family go down with you? Fortunately, the bankruptcy judge allowed him to keep his Manhattan condo so he would not become homeless.

Throughout this book, you will hear more stories from my clients and from my own life about the ways in which the entrepreneurial personality often destroys the very wealth it creates.

ESCAPING FEAR

This is a book for successful entrepreneurs who may or may not see the sword of Damocles hanging above their own heads. People who have the entrepreneurial instinct but need to make sure that instinct brings them happiness instead of pain. People who love to take risks but need to control those risks when it comes to their personal lives.

Unlike most books for entrepreneurs, this is not a business book; it's a wealth management book. Indeed, one of my key goals will be to get you to move your wealth, little by little, out of your dangerous throne room and into a safer place.

Most of my readers will be in their forties, fifties, or sixties. You may be in the midst of your business growth, not yet thinking about your exit from your business. You may have begun trying to plan your exit. Or you may think you love the company you built so much that you will never wish to leave.

For younger readers, this book will not just help you plan ahead but also make sure that as my subtitle promises, you learn how to *develop wealth beyond business and life beyond work.*

Along the way, I will urge you, no matter your age, to move toward what I call a work-optional lifestyle, in which you continue to pursue your entrepreneurial passions while expanding your horizons.

Without fear.

FOR RETIREES TOO

Entrepreneurs who have already exited and retired may not think this book will have anything unique to offer them.

But I have found that my clients who are retired entrepreneurs face special challenges, both psychological and financial. Often, they struggle with the loss of identity that follows retirement from leadership roles. Often, they have to overcome financially risky habits acquired in a lifetime of risk.

Successful entrepreneurs have often established an expensive lifestyle, and when they retire, they will find themselves facing financial stresses they never believed they would encounter when they left the head office behind.

In chapter 2, I discuss the six pillars of wealth management, most of which still apply in retirement—sometimes even more so. Subjects such as wealth preservation, heir protection, and the right way to handle charitable giving are often more important at seventy than at fifty.

A SIMPLE BOOK

As I looked more deeply into the common problems facing entrepreneurial clients, I saw they did not need another complicated book of economic analysis or motivational cheerleading. They needed the basics of sound wealth management, a book that goes beyond mere "financial" management, tailored specifically to their special circumstances and personalities.

You will find this an easy-to-read book that clearly lays out the common challenges and pitfalls facing entrepreneurs and their personal wealth. I want to teach you how to avoid the kinds of mistakes made by my friend Damocles, by my relatives, and by countless other smart businesspeople over the years.

Just as importantly, you will learn how other entrepreneurs have shaped a fulfilling life around the wealth they have acquired—folks who discovered that wealth is not an end unto itself but a means to an end.

THE WORK-OPTIONAL LIFESTYLE

I have already mentioned how I urge my entrepreneurial clients to create a work-optional lifestyle over time. Let me take a moment here to explain that term and why I think it's so important.

From what I've observed among my clients, I think a work-optional lifestyle may be the right goal for most successful entrepreneurs. That's partly because entrepreneurs are not the kind of people who generally like to "fully retire."

You are a restless breed.

Even more importantly, after you get to a work-optional status, you can escape the fear of that hanging sword.

Achieving a work-optional lifestyle means much more than achieving "business success." Owning a successful business does not mean that you have found financial security. As my unfortunate relatives discovered, a change in the business environment can bring a rapid end to any business at any time.

Work-optional means your true *personal* financial success will not ultimately come by growing and stabilizing your business. Your *personal* success will come by developing enough wealth *beyond* your business so that work itself becomes a choice.

When you reach that point, if you decide to continue working your business, you can do so with new joy. But you will also have the freedom to develop the other parts of your life—which, I guarantee, will become vital to you at some point. Even if they aren't just yet.

If you develop sufficient wealth beyond your business, you will have the freedom to participate in the arts, enjoy your family, play golf, go sailing, support charities—wherever your passions lead.

COPING WITH THE ENTREPRENEURIAL PERSONALITY

I don't need to tell you that we live in the great age of entrepreneurs. Technology has enabled new markets to emerge with astounding speed, and new businesses can now reach virtually anyone on earth to solve problems for a profit.

But the real dynamic of our age is rapid change, and change is like oxygen to an entrepreneur. If you are a successful business creator, you are probably one of those rare individuals who see change not as a threat but as an opportunity.

You no doubt *embrace change*, which is a wonderful trait for making businesses thrive.

You are also no doubt *action prone*. You "just do it" and then learn by doing.

You are no doubt *optimistic*—sometimes absurdly so. If you weren't optimistic, you would never have made it this far.

You have incredible *confidence in your own opinion* and hate to second-guess yourself.

THE DOUBLE-EDGED SWORD

All these much-celebrated traits can bring a person tremendous wealth, *but these same traits inevitably put that wealth in danger.*

Your focus on change can keep you from enjoying the benefits of a long-term strategy. That's because short-term moves may create wealth, but long-term strategies preserve it.

Being optimistic, you often ignore dangers. In fact, you often don't even see the dangers, as if you were wearing horse blinders that focused you on your goals.

Your desire to take action can cause you to spend money and effort to solve problems that don't exist.

Overall, I see that my entrepreneurial clients have a

hard time coping with the absolutely crucial differences between creating wealth and keeping wealth. We will discuss those differences in detail and explore the consequences of an entrepreneurial personality more deeply as this book unfolds.

For now, let me just say that running a business requires a hands-on, action-oriented, risk-taking personality. But the people who do best with investing and preserving wealth usually have a hands-off, low-action, low-risk personality.

Perhaps you're beginning to see the problem.

WHY SHOULD YOU LISTEN TO ME?

What qualifies me to write this book? Over a complicated career, I have been a successful entrepreneur, a successful investor, and a successful financial advisor—though only in the last role did I find my true passion.

I started two businesses in China before I emigrated to the United States on a scholarship to Carnegie Mellon University. Fresh out of CMU, I began and tanked my own dot-com during the bubble, losing my first wife in the bargain. It's a story I'll tell you in this book, because it taught me a good deal about the consequences of the entrepreneurial personality.

After my dot-com debacle, I became a weather derivatives trader for PG&E National Energy Group until the Enron debacle. After that, I started my own hedge fund, and I made a great deal of money in that role until I found that it did not bring me happiness or personal satisfaction. In the end, I gave up my hedge fund when a doctor friend of mine was declining in health and about to die. I stepped in to advise his family on their finances, leading to my present career. You can read that tale in my first book, *Physician Wealth Management Made Easy*.

Through my own triumphs and failures—along with the struggles of my clients—I have learned that *business success* does not necessarily lead to *financial success*, and *financial success* does not necessarily lead to *life success*. There's just no way to draw a simple, straight line from one step to the next.

Indeed, entrepreneurs may need the most help moving from each of the above phases to the next. Over the last two decades as a wealth manager, I have listened to their stories to see how they've done it right and how they've done it wrong. My goal with these clients, as with my readers, has always been to help people create simple, flourishing lives free of financial anxiety.

I want to help you create that life too.

HOW IS THIS BOOK STRUCTURED?

You can jump around in this book, but you will get the most out of it if you read the chapters in order.

In chapter 1, we'll explore the special challenges that entrepreneurs face in managing their personal finances, starting with understanding the two basic kinds of entrepreneurs and the specific issues they encounter.

Given the many pitfalls, how can you build a solid financial house *outside* of your business? Chapter 2 offers the six pillars of wealth management, none of which can be neglected.

Chapters 3 and 4 dig down into the specifics of selecting a financial advisor and following through on a well-founded wealth management process. Spoiler alert: stockbrokers and insurance salespeople are not financial advisors.

Finally, chapter 5 discusses the special challenges entrepreneurs face in sustaining their own personal well-being, including maintaining purpose and meaning in their lives during and beyond the working years. It offers strategies for ensuring "life beyond work."

HOW WILL I BE CHANGED BY THIS BOOK?

The first step to enlightenment is awareness.

To bring you more clarity about your own financial life, I must first pierce through your amazing entrepreneurial optimism by making you aware of how things have gone wrong for people just as smart and successful as you. Sometimes really, really wrong.

The second step to enlightenment will be helping you understand the crucial difference between business, wealth, wealth management, and investing. These are entirely different subjects, requiring entirely different approaches. Even a little knowledge of the differences will help you construct a plan for your future.

But as you may already have realized, the ambitions of this little book go beyond finance. As a successful entrepreneur, I want you to find your trajectory not just to financial security but also to a better life.

In that life, I hope you will continue to grow as a person even as you grow your wealth. I hope you will make strong connections to your family and community even as you pursue your passions.

I hope you will escape the sword of Damocles. And when you do, I hope you will be happy.

CHAPTER I

Personal Challenges

We entrepreneurs are different. We don't just see new possibilities; we act on them. That powerful desire to act accounts for our success in business, but it also creates special challenges.

My own story illustrates the point perfectly.

I first realized I had the entrepreneurial spirit back at college in China. I was living on a shoestring budget during my studies. I had a new girlfriend, and I got the idea of taking her to a newly developed tourist spot named JZG, short for the Jiuzhaigou Natural Reserve. JZG was deep in the mountains close to Tibet—a three-day drive from the nearest city, Chengdu, on a very treacherous road. It was remote and romantic, and I'd seen the scenery in pictures. I knew the place was magical and out-of-this-world gorgeous, just like my new girl.

I asked myself, "How can I possibly afford to take her there?" In that question, an entrepreneur was born.

At the time, I was studying at Beijing University. Tuition was free, but I lived on just sixty yuan a month, provided by my father. Using today's exchange rate, sixty yuan translates to about US$9. The national per capita income at the time was about $200 a year. My father made above average, about $360 a year, around $30 a month. You can see why just sending me that $9 each month was a huge burden to him. It provided enough for food but certainly not enough to take my girlfriend to the mountains.

I needed to find work, but what could I do? When other students thought of working while studying, they usually thought of tutoring math or English, but the pay for tutoring was abysmal, around four yuan a day, less than US$0.50. Why was the pay so low? Because the clients had so little money themselves.

When I asked myself the simple question, "Who has money in Beijing?" one answer came immediately to mind: foreign tourists. These tourists had incomes that were typically one hundred times more than incomes in China. No kidding. During the 1980s, the per capita income in the United States was roughly $20,000 a year, which was literally one hundred times the average Chinese person's income.

My timing was perfect. China had just opened up to the outside world, and the 1987 film *The Last Emperor* by Italian director Bernardo Bertolucci, had just become a hit. The movie led to a great wave of people coming to Beijing to see the legendary Forbidden City featured in the film.

I went to Tiananmen Square, where tourists gathered to enter the Forbidden City. When I saw a group of foreigners, I'd approach and ask if they needed a guide. At first, it was scary to approach strangers. Many people turned me down because they didn't know me, but I persevered. I didn't have an official tour guide certificate, but I was a history buff, and I knew my stuff—such as how the emperor managed to sleep with his hundred concubines.

I asked myself, "How should I charge these wealthy people?" I'd researched the minimum wage in America, which was about $3.50 an hour at the time: a staggeringly high wage from my point of view, as I was living on just that $9 *a month*. I approached tourists and told them I would provide "an American level of service for only the American minimum wage." It was a terrific marketing angle. China was emerging from strict Communism, and the level of service was generally very poor. So promising American-level service for American minimum wage made for a nice pitch.

I still remember the first pair of tourists who hired me as

a tour guide. They came from Italy, and it was a struggle for us to communicate in English. I stumbled through that first tour as I did through many that followed until I perfected my delivery.

Working eight to ten hours, and getting lots of tips and bonuses above the American minimum wage, I made up to fifty dollars a day, *much more than my father or my professors made in a month.* All it took was brains and guts. My guts enabled me to stand there and approach total strangers. My brains gave me the insight to charge prices that would make sense to those strangers, not what would make sense in China. In short, I became a true entrepreneur.

TAKING ACTION WHERE OTHERS HESITATE

No doubt you are also a risk taker who would have seen a change such as the 1980s opening up of China as an opportunity. No doubt you are also a person who takes action when others hesitate. No doubt you are also a person who persists against the odds.

Not everyone is like us. Some of my classmates noticed I was making a lot of money by giving tours in Tiananmen Square. A few of them followed me there and tried to do the same. Mostly, however, they gave up after just a few rejections. I earned the money I needed to take my girlfriend to the mountains, and we had the amazing trip I had imagined. That girlfriend became my wife.

Later, however, when I became obsessed with my newfound entrepreneurial spirit and spent all my time attempting to become a billionaire, she became my ex-wife. I'll tell you more of my personal story in time. For now, I just want you to understand what I have come to understand: *the very same traits that brought me successes often brought me failures.*

This book is all about avoiding those failures.

LET'S START WITH TRUE PRIORITIES

I have happily remarried, and I now have two wonderful young children. The joy of these relationships has changed the focus of my entrepreneurial spirit.

Every year, I attend an elite financial conference that brings successful advisors together to brainstorm and bounce ideas off each other. We learn what works and what doesn't and how to choose the right track.

In our last conference, we held a group session to inspire us for the coming year. At the meeting, we were told to respond to the very open question, "What is the priority in this season of your life?" One guy said he wanted to achieve

$100 million of new assets under management. Another said he wanted to make $100,000 more in income. When I heard these numbers, I began to ponder the larger meaning of creating a bigger business and earning more money. Would such goals make it worth missing key moments of my children's lives? My answer was no.

When the group came round to me, I answered that my upcoming priority was to "accompany my kids as they grow up." I was surprised when no one echoed such sentiments.

If I don't walk with my children in this crucial part of their journey, I will lose that opportunity forever. I cannot recover from that loss as I could from any kind of mere financial shortfall. At that conference I had a kind of revelation, and I began to think in far more holistic terms about the entrepreneurial life. I began to formulate my strategies for "wealth beyond business and life beyond work," the goal that forms the basis of this book.

THE TWO KINDS OF ENTREPRENEURS

Entrepreneurs can broadly be divided into two distinct types, which I call *lifestyle* and *enterprise*. It's important to understand which type you are, and it's vital to recognize the special challenges inherent to each.

THE LIFESTYLE ENTREPRENEUR

About 90 percent of people who start their own businesses are lifestyle entrepreneurs. These folks typically excel in a certain skill, but they don't like to be told how to do things by higher-ups. They started their own business because they enjoy being their own boss, and they crave the independence to do things they truly enjoy. Lifestyle entrepreneurs include everything from professionals such as doctors, lawyers, CPAs, and attorneys with their own practices to people who customize cars, open specialty bakeries, or provide ski instructors to local resorts.

A successful lifestyle business may generate a good cash flow and support a nice living standard, but these entrepreneurs are not thinking about making a killing long term through an exit or otherwise.

In fact, generally speaking, lifestyle entrepreneurs don't plan very far ahead. That's because they're deeply involved with the day-to-day of their business in an integral and indispensable way. Rarely do they become adept at maximizing business equity and long-term value for their companies.

Many lifestyle entrepreneurs don't think much about retirement either and often believe they can manage their businesses for the rest of their lives, just because they are doing the work they love. Sometimes they see their work as their lives and don't place much focus on their families and friends. Unlike their cousins, the enterprise entrepreneurs, they may also see their employees as *part* of their extended families.

Unfortunately, their actual families and friends may simply see them as "working too hard."

Despite my personal past in dot-coms and hedge fund management, I am now a very typical lifestyle entrepreneur. I enjoy giving financial advice and feel I can do that for the rest of my life. My work generates a good cash flow. Sometimes I think about growing my business, but as I realized during that conference, I'm not very motivated to do so. It just doesn't appeal to me. I'm very involved with my business, and I'm not at all "exit-oriented." I love my work, but nevertheless, partly thanks to that disastrous first marriage, I am ever aware of my need for life outside of work.

THE ENTERPRISE ENTREPRENEUR

Only a small percentage of entrepreneurs become enterprise entrepreneurs, and they have a very different focus than lifestyle entrepreneurs. The primary skillset of the enterprise entrepreneur is *business*. Indeed, they may have very little skill in the actual operational category of their enterprise. Their goal is to build up a company for scalability and eventual sale. That means a laser focus on maximizing enterprise value along with realizing that value as quickly as possible.

To achieve that kind of focus, enterprise entrepreneurs must take themselves out of day-to-day operations. To create long-term value, they must rise above any particular project and work to build the overall organization, its policies, procedures, and culture. That means they must delegate, delegate, delegate; indeed, if they're doing any hands-on *work*, they are probably not doing their job.

Enterprise entrepreneurs are good at turning a business into a lean and mean machine, but like their lifestyle cousins, they're often challenged in creating wealth outside of the business arena. Indeed, because of the riches they picture within their enterprise, they may be even more challenged in thinking broadly.

"Why bother building up a stash outside of my business," thinks the enterprise entrepreneur, "if I'm planning to exit with ten or twenty million dollars in five or ten years. Why worry about my IRA today?" Indeed, their energy may go much more into creating a stable enterprise than a stable life. This mindset may extend to their relationships with their employees. Unlike their lifestyle cousins, enterprise entrepreneurs may see their employees simply as cogs in their lean machine.

COMMON CHALLENGES FOR ALL ENTREPRENEURS

I've hinted at the personal challenges faced by those with the entrepreneurial spirit. Now let's catalog those challenges in a more systematic way so you can be aware of them throughout your career and especially when you approach your personal wealth management.

It's my hope that this book will travel with you throughout your entrepreneurial journey. I hope you will review the list below from time to time and say, "Oh yes, I still need to watch out for that."

I. RISK-TAKING

The beautiful risk-taking spirit we possess as entrepreneurs also represents our number one challenge. If you don't like to take risks, you cannot be an entrepreneur at all. But as we saw with my friend Damocles, and as we will see in other examples, the tendency to take risks often damages long-term wealth.

Take some friends of mine, whom I will call the Newtons.

These good people are serious enterprise entrepreneurs. They have a government contracting business that provides IT consulting to both commercial and federal entities in Washington, DC. The business has boomed wonderfully, but one day, I learned that they reinvest *all* their money back into their business.

Their sales have grown to almost ten million dollars a year, but they don't pay themselves much in salary, and out of all that revenue, they save only about a thousand dollars a month. Seriously, that's all. And without my nagging, it would be even less.

The Newtons are willing to risk literally everything they have on their business to make sure it scales rapidly and massively. Again and again, I have asked my friends, "What if something goes wrong?"

2. OVERCONFIDENCE

The entrepreneurial trait of overconfidence is closely related to risk-taking. Once again, some overconfidence is probably part and parcel of being an entrepreneur. If you were not unreasonably confident, you wouldn't launch a business. If you had too much self-doubt, you'd probably prefer the security of being employed and told what to do.

But overconfidence often leads to downfall. My friends, the Newtons, are certainly overconfident. Even at ten million dollars in revenue, they forget that they represent a very small business in the government contracting arena and that a rival could easily quash them.

The worst of overconfidence comes when you assume that because you are good in one kind of business, you will be good in another kind of business. It is simply impossible to be good at everything, even for a brilliant entrepreneur like you. I am great with finance, but I know I'd be terrible in, say, the restaurant business. I couldn't open a Chinese restaurant and make it successful, despite the fact that I grew up in China.

Unfortunately, many entrepreneurs aspire to become "serial entrepreneurs," dabbling in one kind of business after another. Rarely does this work out well.

3. AVOIDING FINANCIAL ADVICE

When good businesspeople run an enterprise, they wisely turn to their COO, their directors, and many other experts to cross-check their business ideas. If they have a bad idea, they will be held back by their advisors.

But when it comes to their personal finances, especially after they retire, entrepreneurs too often rely on their own genius to manage their wealth. After retirement, itching to prove they "still have it," entrepreneurs may see financial advisors as somehow less successful people whose advice they do not need.

At that moment, the confidence bred from a lifetime of success becomes their enemy instead of their friend. The lack of advisors holding them back tends to produce more and more risk. All too often, the results are, again, catastrophic.

4. FAILING TO DISTINGUISH *CREATING* WEALTH FROM *PRESERVING* WEALTH

Most entrepreneurs do not understand that running a business and making long-term investments require entirely different skills and approaches.

To build a business, you input not just capital but also intellect and labor. Usually, there's a direct relationship between the amount of intellect and labor you put in and the wealth you take out.

This relationship is just the opposite when it comes to investments. Seriously, the exact inverse. Research has shown that the more activity you put into your investments, the worse results you usually achieve.[1]

Market timing and stock picking are usually just bad ideas. So are the most sophisticated algorithms and strategies. Usually, you would have done better buying a basket of stock and bond funds and holding them for the long term.[2] We'll discuss this further in the next chapter, under the pillar of wealth preservation.

5. NOT RECOGNIZING THE LIMITS OF MENTAL ENERGY

Mental energy is a scarce resource and probably our most precious resource. This resource gets used up during the day. Studies have shown that humans are capable of making about ten good decisions in a day, maybe fewer. If we use up that capacity, we begin to make bad decisions.

As our mental energy becomes exhausted, we begin going

---

1 Brad M. Barber and Terrance "Terry" Odean published a famous study, "Trading is Hazardous to Your Wealth," *Journal of Finance*, Vol. 55, no. 2, (April 2000). The authors note, "Individual investors who hold common stocks directly pay a tremendous performance penalty for active trading. Of 66,465 households with accounts at a large discount broker during 1991 to 1996, those that traded most earned an annual return of 11.4 percent, while the market returned 17.9 percent."

2 Simply holding diversified baskets of stocks for the long term is advocated by savvy investors like Warren Buffett and Jack Bogle. See, for example, Kathleen Elkins, "Warren Buffett and Jack Bogle Agree on the Formula for Long-Term Success: 'Buy and hold,'" CNBC.com, September 18, 2018, https://www.cnbc.com/2018/09/18/warren-buffett-and-jack-bogle-recommend-buying-and-holding.html.

on instinct or reflex. In other words, we don't think about our decisions sufficiently because we just don't have the mental energy to think.

I eat healthy in the morning and pretty lousy at night. Why? Because I make better decisions in the morning when I'm fresh. In the evening, I make lousy decisions because I lack the willpower to make right decisions. It's that simple.

This truth naturally affects entrepreneurs more than most people because entrepreneurs must make important decisions all day long. By the time they get around to making decisions about their personal finances and their family relationships, their mental energy has been exhausted. So they go with their gut.

Unfortunately, the gut is often wrong.

It's worth noting that Jeff Bezos, founder of Amazon—and considered the *richest person in history*—keeps this in mind when he plans his daily routine. "I do my high-IQ meetings before lunch," he said in an Axios interview.[3] "Like anything that's going to be really mentally challenging, that's a ten o'clock meeting." If something important comes up later in the day, Bezos says he puts it off to the next day. "By 5

---

3   Mike Allen, "1 Big Thing: Jeff Bezos' Secrets for Life, Business," Axios.com, https://www.axios.com/newsletters/axios-am-b5017b5f-3f6b-4ca9-9262-884e5f0b8425.html.

p.m., I'm like, 'I can't think about that today. Let's try this again tomorrow at 10 a.m.'"

Bezos adds that he prioritizes sleep and time with his family. "As a senior executive, you get paid to make a small number of high-quality decisions. Your job is not to make thousands of decisions every day," he said in the same interview. "If I make, like, three good decisions a day, that's enough."

We'll talk more about the proper uses of mental energy in chapter 5, when we look at the overall concept of *entrepreneur well-being*.

6. MISUNDERSTANDING THE FUNCTION OF GOALPOSTS

Entrepreneurs are extremely goal-oriented people. Their business goals are tangible and solid: growth, revenue, profit. They think that if they could just reach those goalposts, they'd be happy. Then they'd take time to relax and enjoy family life.

But outside of a sports field, goalposts become tricky. They keep moving farther down the field as you approach them, and they never quite get reached. That means that waiting to achieve any particular goal before you "have time" for happiness, family, and your health will always be a losing game.

Indeed, the best entrepreneurs have learned that happiness and health tend to be *preconditions* for a successful business life. Certainly, they make success easier to reach. The happy entrepreneur is more creative, more productive, and has better stamina. People who develop strong family relationships have learned how to make strong business relationships as well. We'll also discuss the true function of happiness in chapter 5.

7. OVERIDENTIFICATION WITH THE BUSINESS

Along with offering goalposts, business offers a structure for time, relationships, and personal identity. Like so many other aspects of the entrepreneurial life, this structure presents you with another double-edged sword. If you go to work at seven, have lunch with your coworker at twelve, and then stay in the office for another two hours after your employees leave at five, you have fully organized your life around your business. It's likely that when you get home at 7:30 pm, you will lapse into atrophy. You will read the newspaper or watch TV and avoid conversation with others. After all, you've been talking to people all day long!

It's all too easy for this rhythm to become your very life and, worse, your identity. When you go out and introduce yourself, saying, "I'm Chris from MZ Capital," you become identified with your business in the community and even in your own mind. Subconsciously, you *are* your business. Your business is you.

But you are not your business—a fact that sometimes only hits entrepreneurs when they sell out or retire.

I had a mentor I'll call Harry. Harry was a Midwesterner who ran a business making concrete for large-scale industrial uses. He acquired the business when he was only twenty and worked hard for more than thirty years to turn it into a national business. He told me, "All along the way I was happy, I was productive, I loved going to conferences and working long hours."

In his early fifties, Harry sold out for good money, and for a few weeks, he was very happy. But only for a few weeks. Why? He had nothing to do, and his identity as a person suddenly seemed completely lost. He had planned to spend his retirement playing golf, which he had always enjoyed, but now golf seemed pointless. Soon he was on medications and at one point contemplated suicide.

Eventually, Harry went back to work and started up another business. He tells me that this time he intends never to sell out. He wants to build an enduring enterprise that will have an important impact on the community. Even golf has become fun again.

8. NOT ACCEPTING THE FACTS OF AGING

Entrepreneurs can be overconfident about a lot of things, including the longevity of their business acumen. Your skills and the currency of your knowledge *will* decline over time. No one escapes this reality.

I have a friend I'll call Pete who started a data analysis business, which tracked a variety of key industrial trends around the globe. This business required not just a kind of technical genius but also a deep understanding of global markets. After several decades building up his enterprise, Pete sold it to a large UK-based transnational. He worked through the transition, and then he was out, carrying with him a tidy sum.

But Pete could not let go of his baby. From the outside, he watched as it began to languish and lose its global importance. He could see that to the big transnational, his business was just a minor subsidiary, and it didn't get the support it needed. Not to mention that without his experience at the helm, the ship had gone off course.

Now in his late sixties, Pete decided to jump back in. He made an offer to buy back his business, and it was accepted. After all, the division wasn't doing so well for the transnational, and they were probably glad to cut their losses. Unfortunately, Pete didn't have enough money of his own anymore, so he went to a dangerous kind of loan shark for the considerable balance of the buyback.

Pete took charge once again, but he wasn't the old Pete anymore. He had lost his edge as a technical genius, and the technologies themselves had evolved in an entirely new direction, along with the global markets he once knew so well. All his experience had become irrelevant, and soon, the whole enterprise crashed and burned. In the end, Pete lost everything to the loan shark.

The decline in competency over time is simply a reality of human life. Studies show that somewhere between fifty-five and sixty, our mental capacity begins to decrease—increasing the odds that we will make mistakes. By our seventies, the decline is serious.

Very successful people tend to deny this truth and persist in believing they can function as well after sixty as they did when they were forty.[4]

9. NOT PLANNING FOR RETIREMENT

People who work as employees often end up having more

---

4 Mark Miller, "Safeguarding Your Wealth from the Effects of Cognitive Decline," Morningstar. com, September 4, 2018, https://www.morningstar.com/articles/881050/safeguarding-your-wealth-from-the-effects-of-cogni.html.

comfortable retirements than high-flying entrepreneurs. That's because employees are often encouraged to secure their retirement through 401(k) plans, pensions, and the like. In other words, someone else is forcing them to think about retirement and do some planning.

Entrepreneurs, on the other hand, are on their own. Not only are they overconfident about their ability to handle the financial realities of retirement, but as we have seen, saving for retirement usually happens only as an afterthought. Often, they've staked everything on their business.

Worse, entrepreneurs are often absolutely certain they can bounce back from anything, at any age. After all, they've done it so many times before!

But there's a limit to second chances.

Remember that relative of mine who went bankrupt in his eighties? He had built and crashed at least three major enterprises during his career. When the last one collapsed, he had nothing put away because he had always been so sure he could build another company anytime he wanted. At eighty-three or eighty-four, however, that's not so easy. Suppose instead he had religiously taken 10 percent off the table each year during his decades of success?

10. MIXING PERSONAL AND BUSINESS FINANCES

Enterprise entrepreneurs rarely make this mistake, but their cousins, the lifestyle entrepreneurs, often tend to mix their business and personal finances in a way that endangers the preservation of their personal wealth, creates unlimited liability, and may make a business exit impossible.

Take my client Laura, who has a staffing company that supplies a specific kind of specialized personnel to US government agencies. She's a lifestyle entrepreneur who really should be thinking "enterprise."

Laura's from a minority group, and her business benefited greatly from what's called 8A certification, which gives minority-owned businesses preferential contracting treatment for seven years as they start up. The idea is that after seven years, the business will have grown to a point where it no longer needs hand-holding.

Laura's business did grow—by leaps and bounds. When she first approached me for wealth consulting, she was personally putting aside around $100,000 a month in savings. In as little as a year and a half, she had built up a personal fortune of two million dollars, which I worked with her to invest.

Just a few months later, however, she called and told me

she had to stop putting aside money, as her business was going through some tough times. Shortly after that, she began drawing money out of her investments to put *back* into the business. Why? Because she didn't want to fire any employees. Eighteen months later, her two million dollars had dwindled to zero.

What had happened? Laura's firm had graduated from the seven years of 8A certification, and she was no longer getting preferential contracting treatment. She had not acquired the ability to survive without that treatment in the governmental market, and to this day, she has not developed a significant ability to compete in the commercial market.

A big part of the problem is that Laura is playing in a highly competitive field that requires an enterprise approach, but she still operates as a lifestyle business. She has offices in a nice building with a fancy reception area, but she makes all the decisions and handles all the money herself. To this day, she literally sees her personal funds as an extension of the corporate funds and vice versa.

Like many lifestyle entrepreneurs, Laura also saw her employees like family, and she was unable to make the necessary, cool-headed business decision and shut down her company when the contracts began drying up.

When Laura first became aware of what was happening, she should have stopped while she was ahead and kept the two million dollars she'd saved *out of the business.* At the time of writing this, she's battling on, but she's entirely broke.

As we will learn in the next chapter, the best way to ensure an adequate separation of accounts, accounting, budgeting, and savings is to *always* be thinking toward an exit. When you plan for an exit, you automatically begin creating policies and procedures, along with the financial structures to enable wealth beyond business.

It is not easy for the lifestyle entrepreneur to have the discipline to keep personal and businesses entirely separate—I have been guilty of mistakes in this area myself—but it must be done.

STEPPING BACK

In each of these examples, otherwise-intelligent entrepreneurs failed to step back and look at their personal situations as a complete picture beyond their business. Instead, in a very unbusinesslike way, personality and instinct were allowed to rule the day.

In the next chapter, we will begin the work of stepping

back to see the full picture of personal wealth management so we can build a solid structure for your financial house.

CHAPTER 2

The Six Pillars of Wealth Management

An old Chinese tale tells of two families, the Changs and the Lins. These two families did nearly all the weaving for their village. Each purchased cotton from local farmers. Each wove beautiful cloth from that cotton. Each lived pleasant, even prosperous, lives.

Naturally, Mr. Chang and Mr. Lin competed fiercely. Come market day, they vied to outsell each other with the bolts of cloth they had produced over the previous month. The cloth was of equal quality, but somehow, Mr. Lin always had one or two more bolts to sell, so he often came out ahead at the end of the day.

"I don't understand how, every month, the Lins make more

cloth!" Mr. Chang would complain to his wife. "We work so hard, but I sell out by early afternoon while he always has a bit more and makes more money! No wonder they have a finer house and a servant!"

Mrs. Chang would just smile serenely. "Do not fret, dear. We are doing quite well, are we not?"

"Of course I fret!" cried Mr. Chang. "We should be growing our business, not coming up short each month! Perhaps we should hire some workers."

But Mrs. Chang just smiled.

One terrible year, a drought arrived, and the cotton crops failed. Eventually, a dark day arrived when neither Mr. Lin nor Mr. Chang could purchase any cotton at all to keep their looms working.

Mr. Chang came home to his wife nearly in tears. "Come market day, we will have nothing to sell. Indeed, for months there may be no cotton. We will starve."

"Do not fret, dear," said his wife. "We will continue to do quite well. Come and see." And with that, Mrs. Chang took her astonished husband by the hand and led him out to a storehouse at the back of their property, where she unlocked the door to show him hundreds of bolts of cloth, neatly stacked.

"This should get us through at least six months of sales. We will maintain our customers and our income. You see, dear husband, I have been deceiving you. Each month, I secretly put aside one bolt against such a day as this."

Despite their earlier success, the Lins lost all their regular customers and had to fire their servant, sell their fine house, and give up their weaving business forever.

Meanwhile, the Changs supplied their regular customers with cloth throughout the drought. Indeed, the Changs continued to do quite well.

Where did I learn this tale? It was repeated to me many times by my very practical grandmother as a bedtime story when I was just four or five. She seared it into my mind, and I am glad to have the opportunity to sear it into yours!

BUILDING WEALTH BEYOND BUSINESS

Mr. Chang and Mr. Lin were both hardworking entrepreneurs, but only Mrs. Chang invested for the future. Only Mrs. Chang understood that the long term matters more than the short term and that *her family had to build wealth outside the day-to-day profits of their business.* For all of us, good entrepreneurship will never be enough. In the end, all of us must become *investors.* All success brings its own risk and must be protected.

In modern times, one must do more than pack away bolts of cloth in a storehouse, but one must still build the storehouse. In this chapter, we will discuss the six pillars of a strong financial storehouse:

1. Wealth preservation
2. Tax mitigation
3. Asset protection
4. Heir protection
5. Charitable planning
6. Exit planning

Regardless of your present expertise, I urge you to read through each of these sections so you are certain you have thoroughly considered the construction of each of your pillars.

PILLAR I: WEALTH PRESERVATION

Wealth preservation does not mean storing cash away in a safe. If all your money stays in cash, inflation alone will cause it to lose 2-3 percent in value each year. Indeed, as you age, your investments must grow to create enough ongoing income for you to retire. And believe me, whatever you think now, someday you will want *the option* to retire.

BEGIN BY AVOIDING CONFLICTS OF INTEREST

Now, investment is a large topic, and no one book can make you an expert in the subject. I will give you a few basic principles in a moment, but let me begin by saying that because you are a person of means, I want you to work with a qualified financial advisor. Chapter 3 talks about the proper process for working with a good advisor, and chapter 4 will tell you how to select one.

For now, I just want you to understand that most of the financial industry is built on deeply entrenched conflicts of interest, and your number one job will be to spot and avoid those conflicts.

Many "financial advisors" are in fact licensed brokers who are under no legal obligation to put their clients' interests ahead of their own. Their real job is to make as much money as possible from you, as quickly as possible. They are nothing but salespeople.

Again, this does not mean you can do without financial advice. But it does mean that you must approach all advisors, and all their recommendations, with some skepticism. You must develop your own wisdom to evaluate theirs.

This includes the very biggest names in the business. Indeed, the very biggest names may pose the biggest dangers.

YOU MUST RECOGNIZE VOODOO WHEN YOU SEE IT

Indeed, 90 percent of the investment advice you hear from brokers, Wall Street celebrities, and the media doesn't only include a conflict of interest. It also represents *sheer nonsense.*

Call it a malignant kind of voodoo.

You can think about the current state of investing as similar to the state of medicine two hundred years ago. Until the twentieth century, medicine was not a science. It was more of a mystical practice. When people got sick, they went to their priest or shaman or voodoo practitioner, who would pray for them or perform a kind of magic. The "doctors" of the time knew nothing about cause and effect, controlled studies, or peer-reviewed research.

In medieval Europe, these "doctors" would often treat fevers by cutting open a vein and letting out blood. On what basis did they do this? They'd "seen it work" through selective observation. And they could offer their patients high drama.

No doubt such techniques killed more people than the fevers themselves did.

In the last hundred years, medicine has progressed exponentially—but only by evolving from voodoo to science, from faith to evidence.

Investing is just beginning to develop the kind of rigor that medicine developed over the last century. The battle fought by doctors to escape nonsense, hearsay, and chicanery is only now being fought in my own field.

Most of the investment activity found in the brokerages clustered around Wall Street in modern New York City still falls into the realm of voodoo. It's based not on science but on faith. And it's subject to the worst kind of malpractice.

To see voodoo in action, you need look no further than current investment media stars such as the famous Jim Cramer. Such people give enormous quantities of advice on their shows with none of it based on serious research. Like the shamans of old, people like Cramer go by their gut feelings and make their presentations with plenty of "sound and fury," which, as Shakespeare pointed out, generally signifies nothing.

Time after time, these folks' advice has been shown to underperform the general market.[5]

The same can be said of the formulas promoted by countless brokers, fund managers, technical "charters," trend watchers, and celebrity hedge fund rock stars. These people fool you with a false science based on nonsense such as stock chart "double shoulders," "floors," "triple dips," and Fibonacci numbers. The human mind is easily fooled into seeing patterns where none exist, especially under the influence of a voodoo artist. Again and again, such patterns have been proven insignificant and their recommendations as meaningful as white noise—devoid of useful information.

All of these people make a living by promoting the very worst investment techniques: the picking of individual stocks and attempts to time the market. In an average year, 25 percent of money managers outright lose money; 74.76 percent make some money but not enough to overcome their costs. Only a miniscule 0.24 percent of money managers beat the market and overcome their costs to benefit their clients more than the general market. There's no way to predict who these lucky few will be in any upcoming year.[6]

---

5   Jennifer Booton, "Jim Cramer Doesn't Beat the Market," Marketwatch.com, May 16, 2016, https://www.marketwatch.com/story/jim-cramer-doesnt-beat-the-market-2016-05-13.

6   Eugene F. Fama and Kenneth B. French, "Luck versus Skill in the Cross-Section of Mutual Fund Returns," *Journal of Finance*, Vol. 45, no. 5 (October 2010).

CARLOS FALLS UNDER THE SPELL OF A BIG NAME

Carlos is one of the wealthiest citizens in a small Caribbean nation. His story is truly rags to riches, as he started with a small but well-run general store and then expanded and expanded until he was building major shopping malls throughout the islands.

When Carlos came to me, he was worth between $300 million and $500 million, but he was uncertain about his investment brokers. He had set up what's known as a "family office" inside a major Wall Street firm recognized around the world. To someone far from the financial centers of the world, the name was especially impressive. A family office is a nice way of referring to a brokerage team that's 100 percent dedicated to one extremely wealthy family.

When I did an overall portfolio review for Carlos, I was horrified at what I saw. These brokers were basically having a great time gambling Carlos's fortune on high-risk stocks and funds, with over 70 percent of his money in hedge funds. All the while, they were raking in huge fees.

I begged Carlos to tell his family office to at least get out of hedge funds. He eventually listened, but he had already lost millions. Astoundingly, even after these losses, he did not fire his brokerage. He also did not contract with me, as I was just starting out as a wealth advisor, and Carlos no doubt thought, "My private family office in the Wall Street brokerage *must* know better than this young man."

Carlos does check in with me from time to time, mostly to complain about the way his money is handled. Still, the big Wall Street name carries so much clout that he seems unable to break away.

REMEMBER THAT GOOD INVESTING IS
COUNTERINTUITIVE

If you are to escape the voodoo, spot the false gurus, and make wise choices with or without an advisor, you must begin with a few very basic principles, starting with the understanding that *investing is deeply counterintuitive.* The typical wiring of our human brains often misleads us. For example, *it's dangerous to follow the herd.* In most of life, it's safer to follow the crowd, and our brains are wired so that we instinctively seek safety in the herd. When it comes to investments, however, following the herd often proves dangerous.

It's not true that whatever happened this year will probably happen again next year. Humans suffer from a malady known as the "recency bias." As our brain evaluates the possibility of outcomes, we automatically assign more weight to our more recent experiences and less weight to distant memories. If a crash happened ten years ago, it has already become a distant memory. Therefore, we think it less likely to happen next year. But actually, as time goes on, the chance of a new crash increases.

The recency bias has been studied in detail by Daniel Kahneman, a Nobel Prize-winning psychologist, along with other ways in which our psychology affects our economic decision making. He asks, in essence, "How is it that people make the same mistakes over and over again?"

Kahneman's recency bias research works for both good and bad news. If the most recent event is a stock market rally, then we believe that another rally is imminent without any evidence to back up our assumption other than recency.[7]

Ignorant or unscrupulous stockbrokers and other market "gurus" use the recency effect to urge you to "get in now" on whatever has already happened.

Recognize the Problem with Taking Action

After falling prey to voodoo, conflicts of interest, a herd mentality, and the recency effect, the most common error in investing is connected to our predisposition to take action on our investments. This predisposition often leads to trading often and reacting to financial news as quickly as we can. Again, because brokers mostly make money when you *do* things, they will usually lead you down the path to action.

Unfortunately, taking action is most often a bad idea. Indeed, the correct, even if counterintuitive, approach to investing is generally to take as little action as possible.

For example, action-oriented investors often sell a stock and immediately use the money to buy another "better"

7   Daniel Kahneman, *Thinking, Fast and Slow* (New York: Farrar, Straus and Giroux, 2011).

stock. As noted earlier, researcher Terry Odean collected a massive amount of data on these sell-buy pairs, and he found that on aggregate, *the stock that investors sold outperformed the new stock* the investors bought by an average of 2 percent per year.[8]

He also found that on aggregate, the more often investors bought and sold, the more money they lost. Hence, *the people who paid most attention to the market from day to day did more poorly* than those who made long-term investments and let them ride.

In all, research shows that the typical investor gives up about 4 percent a year through poor but easily avoided choices. That means, for example, that an investor could have earned 7 percent over the year through a solid, diversified portfolio held long term. But instead, they earned only 3 percent. With just a small change in investment behavior, they could have substantially changed their lives.

GOOD INVESTING IS VERY SIMPLE BUT NOT EASY

Starting in the 1960s, the advent of the supercomputer allowed the academic world to begin creating a true investment science. Thanks to the abundance of data available in

---

8   Brad M. Barber and Terrance Odean, "Trading Is Hazardous to Your Wealth: The Common Stock Investment Performance of Individual Investors," *Journal of Finance* Vol. 55, no. 2 (April 2000).

the investment world, any theories and practices can now be readily tested against hard historical facts.

A huge body of rigorous research now exists, but it has not been well disseminated to the public. This should not be surprising. Wall Street in particular resists investment science because it proves how most of Wall Street's practices have no value. Hard-numbers academic research shows that, like old-time medical bloodletting, much of what passes for expertise on Wall Street destroys more value than it creates—even while that "expertise" makes plenty of money for the experts.

An entire book could be written about the analysis of investment data and what it has yielded. Indeed, I am working on such a book. The end result of all this analysis, however, is extremely simple:

Hold a diverse, low-cost portfolio, and stay the course.

This advice is extremely simple but not easy for us flighty, emotional human beings to follow. Let's look at each piece and see why.

It's hard to keep investments *diverse* when single stocks provide so much news and excitement. When everyone from bloggers to financial advisors to your brother-in-law eagerly gives you hot tips. But there's pretty much nothing worse than trying to pick individual stocks.

It's hard to focus on *low-cost* investment vehicles when high-cost vehicles are so heavily promoted, often by your own broker (or insurance agent, etc.), and the costs are so carefully hidden. Researchers such as Odean have shown that *cost* (such as fees and loads on many mutual funds) is *the single biggest determinant* of future returns on funds.[9] But hardly any investors even consider these costs and instead look at the completely misleading "past performance" numbers.

Finally, everyone in the financial industry, from brokers to fake financial gurus in the media, tries to prevent you from *staying the course*. The brokers make money from churn, and media gurus make money from creating panics and runs on markets and individual stocks. Unless you learn to be oblivious to this noise, you will not grow and preserve your wealth.

PILLAR 2: TAX MITIGATION

Successful entrepreneurs often employ genuine experts for their company tax planning while ignoring their per-

---

9   Brad M. Barber, Terrance Odean, and Lu Zheng, "Out of Sight, Out of Mind: The Effects of Expenses on Mutual Fund Flows," *Journal of Business* (December 2003).

sonal tax issues until they get close to April 15 each year. You must remember that your personal tax situation will always be crucial to your wealth and requires just as much attention as your business taxes. You should spend some time familiarizing yourself with the fundamental issues, and then you must work with an expert.

PLAN YOUR LIFELONG MOVE FROM LABOR TO CAPITAL

The first thing you have to learn about tax law is that it favors those *with* money rather than those who merely *earn* money. Learn this lesson young, and you will prosper.

America is a proud capitalist country, where capital gains from invested money are taxed at a much lower rate than money from labor. The highest long-term capital gains tax rate is 20 percent, while the highest labor tax rate is around 50 percent—when you combine state, federal, and other taxes.

This difference is stunning, and it's all-important to your financial well-being. *One of the key goals of your personal finances must be to move from labor to capital over the span of your life and career.*

To my surprise, I have learned that far too many entrepreneurs live paycheck to paycheck throughout their careers, saving little outside of their business despite their high incomes. They think that by reinvesting in their businesses and working harder, they will become richer. But earning more through your labor means paying higher and higher taxes. *Work* harder, and usually the government gets a bigger chunk.

The only sure way to become rich is to use your labor to build a decent capital base as early as possible. Don't spend all your hard-won and heavily taxed earned income. Save your money, and then let it make money for you *at reduced tax rates.*

That may well mean restraining your own desires for things such as nice cars and fancy vacations until you have at least $1 million in investable assets *outside of your business* working for you.

CHOOSE COMPANY LEGAL STRUCTURES WITH CARE

The choice of a legal structure for your enterprise will have a dramatic effect both on your personal taxation and your personal exposure to liability. You need to consult an expert, but you also need to learn enough about the issues to oversee your expert.

In the United States, you can organize your company as a

sole proprietorship, a partnership, a limited liability company (LLC), or a corporation.

A corporation may be an "S corp," which literally stands for "small corporation," or a much more formal "C corp," usually used for larger entities. The "C" comes from subchapter C of the Internal Revenue Code.

Taxation is similar for a sole proprietorship, a partnership, an LLC, and an S corp in that the business and the individual are not taxed separately. Instead, all the income from the business flows through to the entrepreneur's personal income, where it is taxed only once on the personal tax return.

A C corp, however, must pay corporate taxes *in addition* to the individual taxes later paid by the entrepreneur when they receive dividends from the company. Importantly, there's a retained earnings limitation on the company as well. The company cannot keep the earnings within the company forever. That means entrepreneurs are often forced to pay themselves dividends, even when that means being taxed twice on the same revenue.

If the entrepreneur opts for a C corp, they're often forced to play a game in which they attempt to zero out the profit within their business by increasing their personal salary or expenses in order to pay no corporate tax at all and thus avoid double taxation. Because of this issue, along with the complex reporting and structural requirements of C corporations, most small businesses rightly opt for an LLC or S corporation structure.

As we will see in the next pillar, asset protection, an LLC additionally offers important liability protections over either C or S corporations.

Sole proprietorships and simple partnerships are rarely good ideas because they offer no protection from personal liability—an issue we will also discuss under the next pillar.

A Caution on the 2017 Tax Reform Act

The Tax Cuts and Jobs Act of 2017, passed under President Trump, did significantly reduce the corporate tax rate on C corporations, dropping it from 35 to 21 percent beginning in 2018. This caused many to wrongly assume it would be beneficial to switch their company to a C corp from simpler structures.

Indeed, the 2017 reform greatly increased the temptation for those with a business to "run their whole lives" through a C corp so as to cut their personal income tax to 21 percent as well.

The IRS is not, however, stupid. It will flag such attempts and can employ, for example, the "excessive retained earnings rule," which means that if you retain more than $150,000 of profits within your business, you will need to justify it.

Also, remember that C corp money remains subject to double taxation, and in the final analysis, 90 percent of entrepreneurs with smaller businesses would still be better off staying with an S corporation than taking on the significant cost, hassle, and burden of switching to a C corporation.

A full discussion of corporate structures is, of course, well beyond the scope of this book. The important point is not to make uninformed assumptions: get the right advice from the right expert who will take into account the full picture of your finances.

SOME INVESTMENTS ARE TAX EFFICIENT AND SOME ARE NOT

After you have money to invest, you must begin to consider the tax efficiency of your investments.

Some investments are tax efficient, and some are not. The difference is crucial, and it can determine the overall success of your investment strategy. Unfortunately, most people don't give tax efficiency a thought when they start placing their money or making trades. And usually, brokers are all too happy to let their clients ignore the underlying tax issues of major investments. They may even go out of their way to obscure those consequences.

Here are the two simple ideas I want you to understand about investment tax efficiency:

1. Investments held for the long term *are taxed much differently* than investments held for less than a year.
2. Tax efficiency can be achieved by *locating* your assets in the right kinds of accounts.

Long-Term versus Short-Term Gains

Tax law specifically penalizes short-term gains with higher rates. Generally, this means assets held for less than twelve months.

Short-term capital gains are taxed as regular income, and the highest federal income tax rate presently stands at 37 percent. As of this writing, there's also an Obamacare surcharge for "rich" folks of 3.8 percent. To that, you can add state income taxes, for a total nearing 50 percent.

If you are in this highest, 50 percent bracket, your short-term gains will be taxed at that same 50 percent. But long-term capital gains are taxed at only 20 percent and only when realized. In other words, if you hold an investment for twenty years, you will be taxed once in twenty years. Would you rather pay 50 percent on gains every year or 20 percent on gains once every twenty or thirty years? It's a no-brainer.

At the individual level, when you make stock market trades, that means you should always hold an asset for at least a year. But generally, the longer, the better.

Is Your Fund Tax Efficient?

Because, as a wise investor, you will hold most of your investments in diversified funds rather than individual stocks, it also matters a great deal whether your fund manager runs a tax-efficient operation. Do your fund managers churn stocks by buying and selling often, or do they hold stocks for the long term?

You can measure fund tax efficiency by looking at the *turnover ratio* of a fund. If the turnover ratio is 100 percent, that means the fund manager turns over all its holdings each year. If it's 200 percent, that means they turn it over twice a year, with an average holding period of only six months. If the turnover rate is 10 percent, then the average holding period is ten years.

I look for funds with a turnover rate around 5 percent,

which means they hold their investments for twenty years on average.

If you make an investment of $1 million in which the baseline return is 8 percent, then in twenty years' time, portfolios holding substantially similar stocks will show very different returns. Invest your $1 million in a fund with tax-efficient investment (low turnover of 5 percent), and it will be worth about $3.73 million after twenty years. The same portfolio invested with low tax efficiency (high churn and turnover of 100 percent or more) will be worth only about $2.19 million.

Locating Your Assets Properly

Investment gains come in two forms: investment income and capital appreciation. These are taxed very differently.

1. Investment income is taxed as personal income every year, in the same way as your labor.
2. Capital gains are taxed only when sold.

Because of this difference, you need to be smart about how you place your investments.

Some investments generate a good deal of annual income but offer low appreciation—for example, a real estate investment trust (REIT). Such investments should be placed in a tax-deferred retirement account, where they will be sheltered from income taxes during your high-income years, with taxes paid only when monies are withdrawn during retirement. After you retire, you will likely be in a lower tax bracket and pay much lower taxes on your profits.

Investments that provide high appreciation should be put in regular accounts because they will be held long term anyway and you will not be taxed on them each year. Again, when you finally sell the investments, you will be taxed at the much lower long-term capital gains rate.

PERSONAL TAX BENEFITS THROUGH YOUR BUSINESS

You can, of course, realize significant tax savings from the fact that you own your own business. Detailing all these possibilities is beyond the scope of this book, and laws are ever-changing.

It's vital, however, to work with a CPA who has specific expertise in helping entrepreneurs find these savings. Selecting this CPA will require some research and should be done in concert with your wealth advisor.

DEFINED-CONTRIBUTION VERSUS DEFINED-BENEFIT PLANS FOR LIFESTYLE ENTREPRENEURS

Much tax mitigation is based on the idea of deferring income from your present high-earning years to your later low-earning years. The deferrals can be done through qualifying plans under ERISA, the Employee Retirement Income Security Act of 1974.

Unfortunately, many entrepreneurs do not fully explore all the available options under ERISA.

Most of us are familiar with qualifying *defined-contribution* plans such as a 401(k) set up by an employer. But a 401(k) severely limits the amount of income you can defer from taxation. There are two parts to 401(k) contributions, those from the employee and those from the employer. The employee contribution is currently limited to $19,000 per year. If the employer adds to that, the total contribution is currently capped at $56,000 a year. As an entrepreneur, you can theoretically get the full amount because you are both employer and employee, but you will likely have to make the same benefit available to your employees.

Contrast that cap with one of the best but most frequently missed opportunities of owning a business—the personal defined-benefit plan. Such a plan can defer taxes and create what amounts to a personal pension.

This option only applies to small, usually lifestyle, businesses in which the entrepreneur does not have employees or in which the employees are much younger than the owner. For enterprise entrepreneurs incorporated as a C corp, other strategies must be pursued.

If you qualify, however, a defined-benefit plan can get you tax deferrals way above the caps imposed by 401(k)s. Why? Because *rather than defining your annual contribution, you define how much money you want to get in your retirement.*

Under a defined-benefit plan, you could say, for example, that you wish to receive $200,000 a year during your retirement. To fund that revenue stream, you would need to have about $3 million by the time you retire. To build toward that $3 million, an actuarial expert might calculate that you need to contribute $200,000 into your defined-benefit plan this year and every year while you are working.

Importantly, this $200,000 will be tax deductible to the business and tax deferred to you.

Setting up a defined-benefit plan is not difficult, but you must utilize a third-party administrator (TPA). Your TPA will then create a plan compliant with ERISA, use actuarial formulas to tell you how much you can contribute each year, and handle the annual reporting with the Department of Labor and the IRS.

Is such an arrangement worth the effort? Definitely. If you are earning $500,000 or more a year, deferring taxes on $200,000 of that can reap enormous benefits long term and ensure that you retire comfortably.

EXOTIC TAX AVOIDANCE SCHEMES

More complicated tax strategies are also available to people who own their own businesses. I call these "exotics." Some of these may be risky from a legal standpoint, especially without the right advice and resources. Certainly the costs in attorney and accounting fees are often not worth the tax savings.

Captive Insurance

For example, larger companies with a minimum of $20 million in annual revenues, and which also face significant risk exposure, might pursue the idea of a *captive insurance* program in which you set up a separate insurance company owned by yourself to which you will pay premiums. Because the first million dollars in premiums to a new insurance company are not taxed, an entrepreneur can theoretically set up a tax arbitrage in which the premiums are written off by the company and untaxed at the insurance company.

This strategy must only be pursued by companies with substantial and legitimate risks that they need to insure and for which they are paying high premiums. It should not be pursued *purely* for tax mitigation purposes, as has often been promoted by people who set these up.

After many legal battles over such schemes, the IRS did establish a safe-harbor ruling in which you can set up a captive insurance company as long as half of its premiums come from a third party, thus proving you are not simply operating a tax dodge.

Complicated? Yes. Worth the risk and setup costs? Get good legal and CPA advice first. Remember, however, that something like captive insurance may be just one legal opinion away from becoming illegal or, at the very least, attracting unwanted IRS attention. The IRS has already said it will consider any captive insurance scheme as a "transaction of interest."

412(i) Insurance Pension Plan

Another exotic tax avoidance strategy is known as the 412(i) insurance pension plan, which was, for a long time, pushed hard by insurance salespeople as a magical way to cut your income taxes and even your estate taxes. In such a plan, a defined-benefit pension is set up using a complex combination of life insurance and annuities.

Like captives, the IRS has labeled 412(i) insurance pension plans as transactions of interest. That means that the IRS says that although such a scheme is not, by its nature, illegal, it will look closely because it has seen many fraudulent arrangements.

As I said, exotic tax avoidance schemes like these are usually not worth the risk and the stress. They put you at the edge of a cliff, and you may fall over that cliff without even being aware of falling. Certainly, exotics will require high fees from attorneys, accountants, and insurance agents.

USE ONLY A CPA WITH A SPECIALTY IN HELPING ENTREPRENEURS

Tax mitigation should never be an afterthought, even for the busiest entrepreneur, but tax mitigation must be delegated. Don't try to do it alone.

Let me repeat that you must use a CPA who specializes in entrepreneurs, preferably one with a long record with many entrepreneurs. Such a CPA will have a far better chance of staying current with the tax laws most relevant to your situation.

Far too many entrepreneurs continue to use a "trusted family CPA" for their personal finances long after they have become successful rather than a specialist who understands the very specific issues they face.

You must also remember that you have a right to a CPA, just as you have a right to an attorney when dealing with the IRS. *If you are ever contacted by the IRS or another tax authority, do not talk to it.* The conversation might head into areas that you have no expertise to discuss, and your words might be used against you. You have every right to tell these authorities to speak only with your CPA.

PILLAR 3: ASSET PROTECTION

Asset protection means preserving your hard-earned wealth from being taken by others in legal actions, justifiably or otherwise.

America is a wildly litigious society. We have just 5 percent of the world's population, but we generate 95 percent of the world's lawsuits. *No kidding, 95 percent.* You don't have to be at fault to be sued. You don't even have to own the asset that injured the other party. You just have to have deep pockets.

Put simply, if you have money, you will automatically attract lawsuits.

GREAT-AUNT ELLEN TAKES THE HIT

Attorneys don't go looking for "fault"; they go looking for pots of money that they can somehow attach to an incident through a "theory of liability." In his excellent book on asset protection,[10] attorney Robert Mintz relates a true, and hair-raising, story that illustrates the situation perfectly. The names have been changed.

A young man named Mr. Fineman runs a stop sign and smashes into a car driven by Mr. Wilson, causing Mr. Wilson a severe injury. Mr. Wilson hires an attorney named Abel. Mr. Abel is a "contingent fee" lawyer, which means he works for a percentage of the ultimate recovery payout. It's a big incentive to go looking for a pot of money.

Attorney Abel sets out to do his research—not legal research into the merits of the case but financial research. He discovers that Fineman has no insurance, no home, and no substantial assets. Abel isn't going to waste time suing someone who can't pay. So he begins looking for someone else who can pay. He asks the following:

1. Was Fineman on an errand for an employer who can be sued?

2. Was Fineman drinking at a restaurant that can be sued for serving him too much alcohol?

3. Was Fineman on medication prescribed by a doctor who

can be sued? Or did he have too much of his meds because a pharmacy filled the prescription improperly?

4. Did Fineman not see the stop sign because some unwitting homeowner failed to trim a tree in front of the stop sign? Or because the municipality failed to position the sign properly?

As Mintz puts it, "In a rational legal system, Fineman would be regarded as the wrongdoer... Instead we have an attorney trying to force the blame onto someone else—who wasn't at the scene and doesn't even know the people involved."

Finally, Abel discovers that Fineman's ninety-two-year-old great-aunt Ellen had purchased the car for Fineman as a gift. Bingo: Aunt Ellen owns a house and has significant savings in the bank.

The result? Great-Aunt Ellen was named as a defendant in the case and was found liable on a theory called negligent entrustment. The jury found that she should not have bought the car for Fineman because she should have known that he was a careless driver. The verdict was for $932,000, and Aunt Ellen lost nearly everything she owned.

Absurd but true.

Why did the jury shaft Aunt Ellen? Mintz puts it this way: "When the contest is between an injured or sympathetic plaintiff and a wealthy or *comparatively* wealthy defendant, the plaintiff will win virtually every time, regardless of the defendant's actual degree of fault."

---

10   Robert J. Mintz, *Asset Protection for Physicians and High-Risk Business Owners* (2nd ed., Bonsall, CA: Francis O'Brien & Sons Publishing Company, 2010).

BUSINESS RISK *PLUS* PERSONAL RISK

As an entrepreneur, you face much more risk of lawsuits than the average person does, and you sit under a truly double-edged sword. You are at risk because you are wealthier than average, but you are also at risk because you have an ownership interest in a business.

In the sidebar on Great-Aunt Ellen, you see an example of how attorneys go looking for pots of money and then come up with a legal theory, no matter how far-fetched, to attach that pot of money to a court action. The newly poor Aunt Ellen is an example of absurd personal liability, but countless similar stories can be found related to any kind of company you can name.

Even if you own a simple ice-cream stand, a customer could sue you. An employee could sue you. A partner could sue you. Your suppliers might choose to sue you. Indeed, anyone remotely associated with your business could find a reason to take you for everything you have.

Do not think that just because you are not at fault, you are safe. Jurors are usually more sympathetic to anyone who has suffered a misfortune than to businesspeople or wealthy people. "Surely," think jurors, "*someone* should pay."

The purpose of the asset protection pillar is to isolate you personally from the liability generated from both your business and your daily life.

PROTECTING AGAINST BUSINESS-ASSOCIATED RISK

Let's start with protecting personal assets from the risks associated with your business. How do you keep your own funds safe when your company gets sued, goes bankrupt, or otherwise faces liability? As with tax mitigation, you must begin by choosing the right legal structure for your business.

Sole Proprietors, Partners, and Limited Partners

If you choose to do business under your name as a *sole proprietor*, you have no personal protection whatsoever from lawsuits generated by your business dealings. If someone goes after your business, all your personal assets are under threat.

If you set up a *simple partnership*, you also have no protection. Indeed, the risk is even higher because every partner is personally responsible for everything that happens in the business no matter who takes the action. If you have one partner, you are responsible for his or her actions as well as your own. If you have one hundred partners, you are liable for the actions of all one hundred.

In a *limited liability partnership, or LLP*, the types of partners are differentiated by risk. You may function as a *general partner* or a *limited partner*. General partners run the business, but limited partners merely provide capital. Let's say I enter a partnership with you to create a fleet of ice-cream carts. You know how to make great ice cream and deploy carts, so you become the general partner. I merely put up a $100,000 investment, register as a limited or "silent" partner, and take absolutely no part in running the company. If one of your carts mows down a pedestrian, *you* may be personally sued if you have not created a more protective legal entity, but *my* liability is limited to the $100,000 of capital I put into the company. It may be possible to remain a limited partner even if I work in the business, as long as I fully stay out of managerial roles.

Still, the risk for all parties remains high.

The bottom line? In most cases, at least in terms of risk, it's a terrible idea to run a business as a sole proprietorship, a simple partnership, or an LLP.

Corporations versus Limited Liability Companies

If you really want to protect your personal assets from business risk, you must establish either a *corporation* or a *limited liability company*, known as an LLC. Remember, however, that from the perspective of risk, the difference is profound, and *your bias should be toward the LLC structure if at all practical.*

The Trouble with "Corporate Veils"

No doubt you have heard of establishing a corporation to "create a corporate veil" between you and your business. Unfortunately, the term "veil" often proves all too descriptive. If woven improperly or not maintained diligently, your own corporate veil will be no more substantial than the old-fashioned lace variety and will be easily "pierced" by an opposing attorney trying to get at your personal wealth.

Indeed, it has become common for a plaintiff to successfully sue a corporation *and* its directors personally at the same time.

S and C Corps Identical from the Risk Perspective

In such cases, it doesn't matter if we are talking about an S corp or a C corp, because the liability issues are nearly identical. The differences between S and C matter a great deal in taxation but hardly at all in personal risk.

Don't make the common mistake of thinking that the more formal C corp provides the maximum separation between you and your business's liability.

The problem with a C corp is that it requires an extremely high burden of record-keeping and corporate formalities, which may be impossible for a smaller entity to maintain. This includes a formal board, board meetings, corporate minutes, regular filings, and much more. Fail to keep the formalities, and an opposing attorney will claim that your corporation doesn't actually exist and that you are personally liable for everything that occurs. Even the smallest lapse may prove your undoing.

How the Veil Gets Pierced

How do plaintiff's attorneys attempt to "pierce the corporate veil" and go after your personal bank accounts, insurance policies, and even your house?

First, they look for evidence that the entrepreneur is using business money to pay for personal expenses. If you've been good with separating these monies, the attorney will next subpoena your corporate minutes to see if you have been holding quarterly meetings and so forth. If you don't have proper documentation, you can find your personal assets fully exposed.

To summarize, the veil provided by a corporation can be "pierced" by an opposing attorney if the following occur:

- You mix personal and business assets.
- You don't properly capitalize your company.
- You don't hold your quarterly and annual board meetings and keep detailed, accurate records.
- You don't do the formalities, such as creating company bylaws.
- Your officers don't abide by those bylaws.

The above list is not exhaustive, but such mistakes are the most common.

THE ADVANTAGE OF AN LLC OVER A CORPORATION

The LLC structure was created when states began to realize that the corporate structure provided insufficient protection to many kinds of entrepreneurs. These states saw that the risk for entrepreneurs needed to be reduced if business was to flourish in our suit-happy nation. The new structure proved so successful that all fifty states now offer the LLC option.

Importantly, an LLC is a *company* not a *corporation.* In short, it allows entrepreneurs to create a company that need not follow all the formalities of a corporation and, in most cases, that is fully protected from liabilities generated by their business. Indeed, the LLC laws specifically bar a lawsuit against an LLC from also targeting the company's managers and members.

Equally important, the burdens of record-keeping are far less in an LLC than in a corporation, and things such as formal board meetings and corporate minutes are not required; hence, you have less exposure for not following the niceties.

Naturally, it's prudent to observe some formality in running an LLC, but the law is quite lenient compared to corporate regulations, and in general, the LLC armor is much harder to pierce. In the last pillar, we also saw how an LLC offers important tax advantages over a corporation.

YOU MAY HAVE "BUSINESS" RISKS YOU DON'T RECOGNIZE

Before we move on to personal protections, I should point out that many people are running high-risk businesses without even realizing it.

Do you own rental property? If your tenant fails to sweep the snow on their walkway and one of their guests slips, who do you think the guest is going to sue? The tenant or you?

Every property rental business should be put inside an

LLC to limit the liability of the owner. As part of the LLC, the rental property itself may be at risk in a lawsuit, but at least your other personal assets will be protected. Indeed, if you rent out three properties, they should be held by three *different* LLCs so a lawsuit against one does not endanger the others.

It could be said that nearly any asset you own can create liability for you. Your business creates a high risk. A rental house brings an almost equally high risk. Your own residence brings lesser but still meaningful risk that requires insurance. Each asset should be examined for its liability and steps taken to protect you from that liability. Fortunately, assets such as bank accounts and brokerage accounts can be targets, but they do not in themselves create risk.

PROTECTING YOUR BUSINESS FROM PERSONAL RISK

Your personal life may also bring legal risk to your business. These are sometimes called outside threats, meaning threats that do not arise from the operation of the business itself, which are known as inside threats.

Suppose I am at fault in a traffic accident in which someone gets hurt and I am successfully sued for a great deal of money. What happens to my business? Can it be attacked for payments? My dividends garnished? Can the company actually be foreclosed or my shares in the company seized? All these are, after all, assets of mine.

Once again, your *sole proprietorship* offers no protection. Its assets are entirely at risk of seizure or even business foreclosure if you are sued personally.

We just learned that a *corporation*, whether S or C, is very weak in protecting you from inside threats. It's entirely useless in protecting from outside threats. Your corporate shares can be seized if you lose a lawsuit. Indeed, if the plaintiff becomes the majority owner of the shares, they may seize control of the corporation itself.

An *LLC* may provide a measure of protection, though not complete protection. How much protection depends on your state.

About two-thirds of US states limit the effect of a personal judgment against you to a "charging order" against your LLC. A charging order means that although a successful plaintiff can garnish your distributions from the company, they cannot threaten the company itself with foreclosure or seizure of company assets. This may allow you to hide your assets inside your LLC so long as you have an operating agreement that prohibits you from distributions in the case of a hostile event. If you have such an arrangement, the LLC can simply stop issuing you distributions.

Unfortunately, another third of states *do* allow the judgment creditor to foreclose on your LLC and potentially seize everything you have in the business.

The same state laws generally apply to LLPs.

It's vital to consult your attorney or CPA so that you understand the situation in your own state and take whatever steps you can to protect your business from your personal risks.

BUILDING FORTRESSES AGAINST ALL KINDS OF RISK

Now let's look at some specific legal fortresses you can build to protect your personal assets from *any* kind of attack—be it from a former business partner, a former spouse, an unhappy neighbor, or an unsatisfied client of your business.

A proper fortress offers a psychological barrier as well as a physical one. If opposing attorneys see that you have placed your wealth inside the right kind of fortress, they will often just give up. If, however, you take no significant measures to protect your wealth, you will make yourself a more attractive target. If your money is "lying right on the ground"—say because you are keeping it in a simple bank account under your own name—you can be sure that even if you have done nothing to justify lawsuits, you will attract lawsuits.

Attachments and Liens, Even during a Suit

Few people realize that their personal assets are at risk even *during* a lawsuit, well before any judgment is rendered. A plaintiff's attorney may ask the judge to place an attachment or lien that freezes your bank accounts, brokerage accounts, or any other assets under your name while the trial is going on.

This powerful weapon can do more than weaken your legal position; it can make your life miserable. You may not even be able to pay your attorney to fight back, making it impossible to win the lawsuit, even if you have a good case.

LLCs as Asset Fortresses

If you consider yourself at risk, consider creating LLCs to hold your bank accounts, your brokerage accounts, your house, or any asset. Even though the LLC technically owns these assets, you can maintain full access to your resources.

As we have seen, assets inside an LLC may not be fully

protected from a judgment, especially in states that allow successful plaintiffs to force a foreclosure of the company. But an LLC *does* put your assets beyond the reach of attachments and liens during a legal action. Until your opponent wins, they cannot tie up your resources.

Indeed, an LLC may be just the psychological edge you need to discourage an opposing attorney from trying a lawsuit at all.

As always, make sure to do your homework with your own qualified attorney.

Privacy Trusts

If an opposing attorney can't find information about your assets, they cannot or will not launch a legal attack on you. If your real estate assets are under your name, those assets are just a quick title search away. What about your banks and brokerages? Can they be counted on to keep your information private? The answer is absolutely *no*. Whatever privacy rights you had to your financial information all but vanished after 9/11 and the beginning of the war on terror.

One solution may be placing all your most important assets in what's known as a *privacy trust*.

In such a trust, your name nor your address nor your Social

Security number will be directly connected to your assets. If you open a trust with XYZ Trust Company, and your trust name is XYZ Trust 12345, you can title your house to XYZ Trust 12345, and you can put your bank and brokerage accounts under the ownership of XYZ Trust 12345 as well. The corporate trustee will execute on your behalf according to the trust document, and your identity will be concealed.

Well, perhaps.

A privacy trust makes it much harder, but not impossible, for the opposing attorney to get hold of your asset information. If by some means—say a mole in the trust company—the opposing attorney finds out that XYZ Trust 12345 is linked to you, then all bets are off. If you lose the lawsuit, the privacy trust will not by itself protect your assets from seizure.

Asset Protection Trusts

A privacy trust simply helps keep your sensitive financial information away from prying eyes; beyond that, it offers no actual legal protection.

Greater security may be offered by an *asset protection trust*, which does provide a measure of legal protection. In states or countries that allow asset protection trusts, assets can be legally kept from the reach of creditors while you continue to enjoy the fruits of those assets. Many asset protection trusts also incorporate privacy trusts features to help hide your assets from predators.

Asset protection trusts may be domestic or foreign. The differences are substantial.

Domestic Asset Protection Trusts

Many Americans would like to keep their assets protected from creditors while continuing to live on the income or principal of the assets. They'd also like to keep their assets within the United States, where they can be accessed more easily.

American legal traditions have generally frowned upon such arrangements because they might encourage unscrupulous behavior and destabilize the business environment. That's why, until recently, asset protection trusts existed only in small, money-haven countries, such as the ones in the Caribbean islands.

In the last decade or so, however, some smaller or less populous US states became envious of the money flowing to offshore havens and began to enact new laws. As of this writing, the following states allow some form of asset protection trusts: Alaska, Delaware, Hawaii, Mississippi, Missouri, Nevada, New Hampshire, Ohio, Rhode Island, South Dakota, Tennessee, Utah, Virginia, West Virginia, and Wyoming.

The advertising for these arrangements can be a little misleading, because such trusts may not be entirely secure.

Let's say you live in Nevada, the plaintiff is in Nevada, and the court case is in Nevada—a state that allows asset protection trusts. Then yes, a Nevada asset protection trust might help *as long as the case does not go to federal court.*

What if you live in Maryland and the court case is in Maryland, a state that does not recognize asset protection trusts. Would a Nevada trust protect you? The answer is likely not at all.

There's also a federal law that limits these types of state arrangements. Without getting into details, this law says that unless you put the money in the trust far in advance of any lawsuit, you cannot hide that money. The feds don't let you say, "I'm likely to get sued in the next year, so let me create a domestic asset protection trust." And of course, in such cases, federal law overrules the states.

Importantly, the status of domestic asset protection trusts is ever changing at both the federal and state levels. Proceed only with great caution.

Foreign Asset Protection Trusts

For those with very substantial assets and exposure, the most secure fortress is a foreign asset protection trust in which you literally move your money to a small country with better trust protections than the United States. If you establish a trust in the Bahamas, a US court may render judgment, but the Bahamas will be under no obligation to carry out that judgment.

Why do these secure offshore trusts exist? Places such as the Bahamas have fewer concerns with encouraging local business than with trying to attract money from overseas. So they have created laws that allow you to benefit from a trust in their country that is completely protected against your creditors. Indeed, US attorneys sometimes create complicated arrangements in which your trust money hops from island to island in the Caribbean as a plaintiff's attorney chases it until the plaintiff exhausts their resources.

I do not, however, generally recommend foreign trusts to my clients. Foreign trusts require an enormous amount of work and are generally not necessary. Unless you have liquid assets totaling over $10 million and face a very serious risk, it's unlikely that the specialized, expensive attorney and considerable effort would be worth the added safety. After your money has been moved, you will also find it extremely inconvenient to access it, and you might incur continuing legal costs just to maintain that access.

Charitable Trusts

One powerful but often-overlooked vehicle for asset protection is the irrevocable charitable trust. I offer a full discussion of charitable trusts under the charitable giving pillar. For now, let me just point out that if it is structured correctly, you can often benefit personally from the assets otherwise "locked" into a charitable trust while those assets are fully protected from creditors, opposing plaintiffs, and other predators.

In a CRT, or charitable remainder trust, for example, you could grant the trust substantial assets and live off the income from those assets, as long as a certain "remainder" goes to charity when you die—all while those assets remain safe from lawsuits.

SIMPLER ARRANGEMENTS

For many entrepreneurs, far simpler arrangements that require no attorneys, LLCs, or trusts, may be sufficient for your personal assets. Indeed, a few basic precautions can go a long way to address asset protection. Sometimes with just 10 percent of the effort, you can accomplish 90 percent of your goal.

Once again, the situation varies greatly by state.

Tenants in the Entirety

For example, in about half of US states, your money can be protected simply by putting it into an account structured as "tenants in the entirety" with a spouse. Usually, bank accounts are set up only as "joint tenants with rights of survivorship," but mere joint accounts with or without rights of survivorship offer no asset protection and are vulnerable to suits.

Accounts with tenants in the entirety (or similar language) offer the possibility of making your assets inseparable from your spouse's ownership. How does this protect you? Unless your spouse somehow participated in your actual actionable event—say a mistake you made at work or a traffic accident—he or she cannot be named in the lawsuit as a defendant, and your joint assets cannot be pulled from the account for a settlement.

Say you are a successful surgeon and your husband is a

flight attendant. If you are sued for actions you took in the operating room, the plaintiff's attorney can try to go after your bank accounts. But if an account has been structured as tenants in the entirety, *your spouse also owns the account in its entirety.* Hence, unless your husband took time off his job to hand you scalpels, this account cannot be attacked.

Obtaining this protection may be as simple as checking the right box when you set up the account. But once again, the precise naming of such accounts, along with the associated protections, varies by state, so you must do your homework. And get the advice of an in-state attorney or accountant.

Below you will find a list of states currently offering tenants in the entirety.[11]

---

11   Mary Randolph, "Avoiding Probate with Tenancy by the Entirety Ownership," Nolo.com, July 14, 2017, http://www.nolo.com/legal-encyclopedia/free-books/avoid-probate-book/chapter6-4.html.

STATES WITH TENANCY BY THE ENTIRETY OF OWNERSHIP

ALASKA*	MISSOURI
ARKANSAS	NEW JERSEY
DELAWARE	NEW YORK*
DISCTRICT OF COLUMBIA	NORTH CAROLINA*
FLORIDA	OHIO ‡
HAWAII	OKLAHOMA
ILLINOIS**	OREGON*
INDIANA*	PENNSYLVANIA
KENTUCKY*	RHODE ISLAND*
MARYLAND	TENNESSEE
MASSACHUSETTS	VERMONT
MICHIGAN †	VIRGINIA
MISSISSIPPI	WYOMING

* FOR REAL ESTATE ONLY
** FOR HOMESTEAD PROPERTY ONLY
† JOINT TENANCY OF HUSBAND AND WIFE IS AUTOMATICALLY A TENANCY BY THE ENTIRETY
‡ ONLY IF CREATED BEFORE APRIL 4, 1985

Protecting Your Home

You may be shocked to learn that in many states, your personal home may be a highly vulnerable asset in a lawsuit. In other states, your home may be protected from seizure under a "homestead exemption."

As of this writing, Florida, Iowa, Kansas, Oklahoma, South

Dakota, and Texas have laws protecting 100 percent of your home's equity—assuming you follow all the rules. Other states may offer limited homestead protection. Some states, such as New Jersey and Pennsylvania, offer no protection at all.

In any case, the amount of protection and the related rules are varied and ever changing. For example, in New York, the degree of protection changes county by county.

One simple way to protect your home is to take out a home equity loan. Such a loan immediately makes your home a less attractive target because it is being used as collateral to a bank. The bank holds a lien, so a plaintiff's lawyer would have to fight not only you but also the bank. Suddenly, you have a very strong partner at your side—a partner with excellent legal staff.

A smart plaintiff's attorney might quickly find it not worth their effort to fight both you and the bank. Even if they were to win, they know it's likely that not much cash would be realized by taking your home.

Just establishing a home equity line of credit (HELOC) might be sufficient to deter a lawsuit. You don't even need to take any money out through your HELOC.

Again, consult a qualified in-state attorney.

Retirement Accounts

The different kinds of retirement accounts may or may not offer protection against attack by a plaintiff's attorney.

In general, employer-sponsored plans, such as 401(k), 403(b), and defined-benefit plans, are covered under ERISA and are fully exempt from creditor claims by federal law.

The protections offered by an IRA depend on your state of residence. Although most states do protect IRA accounts from creditors, there are a few states that either don't or provide only partial protection.

Again, you must do your homework, work with a qualified in-state attorney or CPA, and make sure your retirement accounts stay protected.

LIFE INSURANCE AND ANNUITIES

In the next pillar, I will explain how life insurance and annuities are often horrible investments. Some states, such as Florida and Maryland, do provide 100 percent protection against seizure of your life insurance annuity by a plaintiff in a lawsuit, however.

In another state, you may not be so lucky. In some, for example, only the first $6,000 of an annuity may be protected from lawsuits.

UMBRELLA INSURANCE

Everyone with significant assets should, however, carry an umbrella insurance policy, which can protect you against a wide variety of liabilities and lawsuits, including things like excessive damages from car accidents.

Umbrella insurance is generally inexpensive and may cost you just $50 a year for $1 million in coverage.

PILLAR 4: HEIR PROTECTION

No one can guarantee that you won't be run over by a truck tomorrow. But if it does happen, don't you want to be run over with peace of mind?

I'm joking, but as a person with significant assets, you do have a special responsibility to make sure that your spouse, your children, and your other dependents are well taken care of when you are gone.

My own wealth management business was founded when my rather wealthy doctor passed away and I was called on to help his surviving family untangle a mess and make the necessary financial adjustments—all because he had done no proper planning. Again and again, I have witnessed firsthand how poor planning places an enormous and unnecessary financial and emotional burden on loved ones.

UNDERSTANDING THE BASICS

For starters, it is crucial to know that you need much more than a mere "last will and testament."[12] Your to-do list may include establishing a trust, designating guardians for minors, giving careful thought to tax issues, planning for the unexpected succession of your business, establishing powers of attorney for others if you are incapacitated, general planning for disability as well as death, and the creation and maintenance of complete financial records.

You also need to take into consideration the special issues in your state, as well as special issues your heirs may face, such as educational expenses, unstable marriages, or complex tax issues of their own.

To establish a proper trust and account for all these complexities, you *must* hire a specialized estate attorney to draft your documents. This must be *an attorney in your state* with

---

12   Except, perhaps, in Texas. In Texas, a will carries surprising weight, and the process has been significantly streamlined compared to other states.

a deep knowledge not just of estates but of tax issues and asset protection. Do not depend on a "general purpose attorney," and don't even think about using downloadable trust templates or generic internet services to do this right.

Let's look at some of these issues just a little more closely.

Avoiding Probate

Your number one goal should be to protect your heirs from going through probate court. This process can easily take more than eighteen months, even in a simple situation. It exposes *all* your assets to public view and subjects your heirs to a chaotic, expensive, and highly confusing legal maze. It may also lead directly to conflicts between your heirs and attacks by creditors and shysters of all kinds.

Unless you have a well-constructed and carefully maintained trust with clear instructions to your successor trustee, probate is inevitable. *Again, a will is never enough.* Indeed, a "last will and testament" is nothing but a piece of paper expressing your desires to a judge who will ultimately decide the fate of your assets—usually in just a few minutes of deliberation.

The Trust

For most people, the appropriate vehicle for the transfer of assets is a "living trust," but do not assume a living trust is right for you, and one size definitely does not fit all. There are revocable and irrevocable trusts, grantor-retained annuity trusts, "intentionally defective grantor trusts," and many more flavors to consider. Only a qualified estate attorney can help you design a trust to achieve your multiple purposes—from asset protection to tax mitigation and from charitable planning to managing the resources of minors.

After you create a trust, you must move your assets into that trust during your lifetime and while you are still mentally competent. While you are alive and competent, you control the trust. Later, control passes to the trustees (usually heirs) you designate.

If you have property in multiple states, creating a trust becomes even more important. Without a trust, your loved ones will not only have to go through probate *but also have to go through probate in each state separately.*

Remember, however, that IRAs, 401(k)s, life insurance, annuities, and any account designated as TOD (transfer on death) to specific persons cannot be included in a trust. They are, however, included in the deceased's estate and subject to estate taxes.

The Pour-Over Will

The companion component to a trust is something known as a pour-over will, which makes sure that whatever assets you did not move into your trust will be "poured" into the trust at the moment you die. For example, if you neglected to make your trust the owner of your car, the pour-over will can remedy your oversight. Your heirs will not have to go to court just to get control of your car.

Advance Healthcare Directive

An advance healthcare directive says, "If I am incapacitated, these are the instructions to my family and my physicians." Often, this means giving your loved ones permission to end life support if you fall into a vegetative state and cannot make decisions for yourself.

Without such a document, decisions that need to be made by your loved ones will be far more painful. This document also generally gives someone your "durable power of attorney for healthcare decisions."

Durable Powers of Attorney: Personal and Business

You will also need to create a more general durable power of attorney. Despite its confusing title, this document has nothing to do with your attorney. Instead, it gives certain powers to someone you determine who can conduct business on your behalf if you are incapacitated or even, say, unreachable while out of the country. This may be your spouse, your child, a sibling—anyone you trust. Everyone over eighteen should give power of attorney to *someone* who could, for example, write checks to utilities on their behalf if they were unable to do so themselves.

As an entrepreneur, however, you may also want to create an entirely *separate* power of attorney for a qualified person to make your decisions related to your company.

MINOR CHILDREN

Anyone with minor children certainly needs estate planning right away. Your will must nominate guardians for young children if something should happen to you and your spouse. Without such a nomination, a court will step in and make its own judgment, possibly placing your children in the care of someone you would not have chosen at all.

You must also deal with the complex questions of how your assets would be handled if you and your spouse were gone but all your children had not yet reached the age of eighteen.

Often, this means nominating a guardian for the children and a separate guardian for your assets, supervised by the court. Making the proper arrangements in advance will be crucial to ensure honesty and prudence by everyone involved.

Any nominated guardian would have to be approved by a court at the time of your death, but courts will generally honor a reasonable nomination.

PROTECTING YOUR HEIRS FROM PREDATORS

Good estate planning must also take into consideration the special circumstance of your adult children. You need to think about the consequences to those children of suddenly inheriting substantial assets or even a business. You must plan appropriately, and you must change that planning as their circumstances change over time.

For example, does one of your children have an unstable marriage that might someday end in divorce? You may want to establish a special kind of trust that will protect their inheritance in the case of a divorce. Indeed, suddenly inheriting a great deal of money is often a *trigger* for divorce, as the divorce will be made financially feasible, or an unhappy spouse may seek a financial windfall in separating.

Does one of your children face bankruptcy? If they suddenly

inherit assets during the bankruptcy process, all of their bequest may end up in the hands of creditors.

Is one of your children irresponsible with money? As you would for a minor, you may want to set up a trust with a separate, responsible trustee who will be empowered to dole out the money to such a child slowly over time. If you have very large assets, you may want to do this even for a responsible child who could not suddenly handle millions.

BUSINESS CONSIDERATIONS

An entrepreneur has a special responsibility to ensure a clear, smooth transition of power if they die or are disabled while still in command of their business. Suppose you owned 50 percent of a business with a partner and you were to suddenly die or become mentally disabled in a car accident. Who would now control your 50 percent? Your spouse? Your child? Are either of those people equipped to make equal business decisions with your partner? What if you are a 75 percent or 100 percent owner?

The circumstances of each business are different, but planning for key person succession is crucial. You might, for example, work with an attorney and an insurance agent to establish a buy-sell agreement in which the business would have the right to buy out your heirs for a specified amount. The capital for that buyout could be arranged through key person insurance.

CLEAR DOCUMENTATION FOR HEIRS

Far too often, heirs are forced to dig through desks, hunt through shoeboxes in closets, wait for statements to arrive in the mail, and otherwise struggle to put together a picture of their parent's—or even their spouse's—finances. In the case of an entrepreneur who passes away or becomes disabled, this effort can be especially daunting.

Billions are abandoned to banks and other institutions each year simply because heirs don't know about an insurance policy, a bank account, an offshore investment, a stock fund, a property, a storage facility, a safe deposit box, or other asset.

It is absolutely your responsibility to keep and maintain up-to-date records and instructions for your heirs. Because your situation probably changes rapidly, you should review those instructions quarterly and make sure your heirs and successor trustees know where to find them.

TRANSITIONAL SERVICES AT THE TIME OF CRISIS

You should also consider working with a professional who can provide crucial transitional services to your family in a crisis. An attorney can only advise on legal issues, but good financial advice—and action—at the right moment might mean everything to your loved ones.

People who have suffered a major loss are in no condition to process the mountain of paperwork a death or significant incapacity produces, especially the death or incapacity of someone with major assets and responsibilities.

Unfortunately, only the rare financial advisor provides the complete range of services your family might need in such a moment. When you are interviewing potential advisors, look for someone capable of assuming this burden after you die.

He or she must be proven in this capacity and must care enough about their work to carry the burden properly. You must not, of course, choose an advisor of your own age or older, who may themselves be retired or have passed on when needed most.

PLANNING FOR DISABILITY

It is four times more likely that your heirs will have to take over your finances or control of your business when you become disabled than when you die. Your disablement will also be a much higher burden on them than your death. Death is a far cleaner event than incapacity, especially mental incapacity. Not only will you become a huge burden, but questions of ownership and control also will be confusing and daunting.

Disability must be part of your business planning, your asset planning, your insurance, and your trust. Again, you must work with a specialized attorney to get the paperwork right.

WHEN DO YOU ACTUALLY NEED LIFE INSURANCE?

Often, I find that entrepreneurs have completely neglected estate planning but have purchased hefty life insurance policies, thinking that they have now protected their heirs.

Like most people, these entrepreneurs usually have a confused understanding of life insurance. Not surprisingly, this confusion is fostered by the lucrative insurance industry.

Often, people mistakenly see life insurance as an investment product or a form of asset protection.

Insurance *can* play a vital role in protecting your heirs when young. And as we have seen, it can also play a vital role in business partnerships. Depending on your state, it can also be a tool for protecting money from predators.

But wealthy people are often targeted by insurance agents for the wrong type of insurance. Often, these permanent policies are very, very expensive and cover the wrong kinds of risks—even nonexistent risks—while creating lifelong monetary obligations.

Let me make this as clear as possible. *Life insurance is a contract to hedge against the financial risk to dependent heirs in the event of the untimely death of their financial provider*—with emphasis on the word *untimely*. In the context of one's family, it should serve no other purpose.

As of this writing, I have two young children. When they were born, I bought a $1 million term life insurance policy on myself to benefit my wife and kids if I died suddenly. Because I was young and healthy, it cost me just $150 a quarter, about $600 a year. I did not see this insurance as an investment; I saw it as managing risk.

If I educate my children well, when they reach maturity, they will not be dependent on me financially anymore. Hence, I will no longer need life insurance to protect them. Put simply, term life insurance for the first twenty to twenty-five years of a child's life is important—*a limited term during which I must pay premiums*. After that, it can play no useful role.

Of course, if a child has special needs, he or she may always be a dependent, in which case, I do help my clients shop for whole life insurance (see the following sections)—one of the rare occasions in which permanent policies make sense.

Insure a Child's Life? Seriously?

Incredibly, sometimes an insurance agent will sell a policy *on a child's life*. This is absurd, as your children have no dependents.

Working adults who support themselves are sometimes even talked into insuring their parents' lives, at high cost—a very poor investment and a hedge against a nonexistent risk.

To protect a nonworking spouse, you should carry *term life insurance* until you accumulate enough assets so that your spouse could survive comfortably if you had an untimely death. Indeed, at the risk of sounding cavalier, a young, educated spouse with job skills or the capacity to remarry would likely find another way to survive without a hefty insurance payout.

Whole Life, Universal Life, and Permanent Life Policy Scams

Permanent life is a broad term that includes both whole life and universal life insurance policies. Either way, this insurance is designed to persist through your entire life.

For most people, that means long after the insurance is actually needed.

Whole life contracts are rigorous. You must pay certain premiums your entire life, with a specific, promised death benefit when you die. Fail to make the payments each month, *and you risk losing your entire investment.* In what other investment vehicle must you play such a dangerous game?

Universal life offers more flexibility, but it often proves an even worse deal. With universal life, you can say, "This month I cannot pay so much, so I'll pay less. A few months from now, I'll catch up." However, the contract also gives the insurance company more flexibility, potentially allowing it to play games with your benefits and wriggle out of the deal. You should not be surprised that insurance companies have structured these contracts so that the advantage usually flows to them.

Insurance agents try to sell young parents whole life or universal life policies on the theory that these are long-term retirement investments and some kind of fund for their children's futures. In truth, however, permanent life policies are usually terrible investments that manage the wrong kind of risk.

Indeed, such policies generally hedge against a risk that does not exist.

Why do agents push these bad deals? Because whenever an agent lands a new permanent life contract, they typically take home 100 percent of the first-year premium themselves—$10,000, in the case described in the sidebar. After that, the agent usually receives 3-5 percent a year, as long as the contract is in force—which might mean the rest of your life. Of course agents push these big packages and lifetime commitments.

As previously noted, for my clients with children with special needs, I do often help them shop for a whole life policy, *as opposed to universal life.* Twenty-five years from now, the child will still be a dependent, even forty years from now. At least with whole life, the contract will rigorously ensure that the insurance company fulfills its end of the bargain. The company will be locked in, not just my client.

In most cases, however, the enormous sums of money dropped into a permanent life insurance policy should instead be invested properly for the future of both the entrepreneur and the entrepreneur's family.

Insuring the Life of a Business Partner

Another important use of whole life insurance involves business partnerships.

AN ESPECIALLY BAD UNIVERSAL LIFE DEAL

In most cases, universal life policies are astoundingly bad deals. Here's a real-world example.

I had a client whose father had bought a universal life insurance policy twenty-three years earlier. The premium was $10,000 a year with a promised death benefit of just $500,000. Over those twenty-three years, the father had paid out a total of $230,000. But despite the fact that the insurance company had been using and investing that money for more than two decades, the "cash value" of the policy was only $150,000. Meaning if he withdrew the money immediately, that's all the father would receive.

But the story gets much worse. This universal life policy allowed the company to charge a "mortality cost" against the cash value, levied each year. When the father bought the policy, he was just fifty-two. Now he was seventy-five, and because his chance of dying had risen considerably, so did the "mortality cost"—hitting $50,000 a year. Of that money, $10,000 was coming out of the premium and $40,000 out of the cash value of the policy.

What does that mean? In less than four years, this $40,000 charge would have completely destroyed the cash value, and when the cash value was gone, the policy would have lapsed. In other words, the approximately $270,000 paid into this so-called "permanent life" policy would have been given to the insurance company as a gift.

Only if the father died in less than four years would the son receive any death benefit at all. Hard to believe but true.

I managed to renegotiate the policy, reducing the death benefit to $300,000 and therefore lowering the mortality cost. In that way, the $10,000 annual premium, if paid, would continue to support the policy for another fifteen years. But it remained a staggeringly bad deal.

A good business partnership will include a buy-sell agreement with a provision for an insurance settlement to buy out a surviving spouse.

Suppose the business has a total value of $2 million. If one of the business partners dies, the business would get $1 million from an insurance policy to buy out the surviving spouse—who would inherit the money instead of the shares. The insurance itself will be a deductible business expense with a tax benefit. If the partnership has a known termination date, then the business would buy term life instead of whole life.

Never Buy More Insurance than You Need

The bottom line on insurance? Never carry more than you need. You should evaluate your risk on a regular basis, and you should seek advice from an independent financial advisor, not an insurance agent with an inherent conflict of interest.

PILLAR 5: CHARITABLE PLANNING

Every wealthy individual, regardless of their present charitable intentions, should have a solid understanding of charitable planning. That's because *long-term* charitable planning can dramatically save on taxes during your high-income years and maximize your charitable impact later on.

The problem is simple but often ignored: for most people, their high-income years do not coincide with their high-giving years. Your forties and fifties are usually your high-income years. But people generally become more charitable after they retire, have time for charitable work, and know that they're financially secure. That's why the charitable years usually come in the sixties and seventies.

This disparity in time frame creates significant financial issues.

THE DONOR-ADVISED FUND

The simplest vehicle for long-term charitable planning and maximizing tax benefits is the donor-advised fund. Designed for the merely wealthy and the not-so-wealthy, it's convenient, easy to set up, and easy to administer.

I typically use a donor-advised fund to help my clients save taxes now as well as save for their future charitable donations. *With this vehicle, your actual donations may not occur until twenty years from now, but the tax benefits can be realized today, when you're in your highest tax bracket.*

A donor-advised fund works like a much simpler version of a charitable foundation—which we will discuss later—but with no dedicated staff and minimal overhead. After it's created, you can, for example, donate $10,000 to the fund every year. The $10,000 is deductible in that same year, even though it has only gone into the fund and not yet to a specific nonprofit. You may choose to give away $3,000 of that money this year, but the other $7,000 will stay in the fund and grow until you are ready to give it to a charity, perhaps during your retirement.

If you do not set up such a fund or other vehicle and you wait to make these donations until you are in your sixties and seventies, you will have no significant income against which to take a deduction. That means you've lost some of the most important write-offs you might ever have taken.

Any large, reputable investment company such as Fidelity or Vanguard can set up a donor-advised fund for you. Then a financial advisor can find other ways for you to maximize both deductions and contributions.

For example, when I contribute to my own donor-advised fund, I usually contribute an appreciated asset such as a stock. In that way, I can avoid capital gains taxes but still get the full amount of the tax deduction for the full value of the stock. Both the charity and I become winners.

Suppose I bought a stock for $5,000, and it has increased 100 percent over time, so it's now worth $10,000. If I sell the stock and then contribute the money, I will have to pay about 20 percent, or $1,000, in capital gains tax. Then I can donate only $9,000 to the charity.

If, on the other hand, instead of selling the stock I donate it to my donor-advised fund, I avoid the $1,000 in capital gains taxes, and I have provided $10,000 in value to the fund. In addition, because my combined federal and state tax rate is almost 50 percent, I will get about $5,000 in tax deductions. Net result? I gave away $10,000 in charity and saved about $6,000 in taxes.

With my donor-advised fund, I almost feel as if I have my own charitable foundation—and it's a great feeling.

Even if you don't see yourself planning for big donations later in life, you may be giving pretty regularly to a church, a synagogue, a mosque, or another nonprofit. Sitting down with a good financial advisor and tax planner can properly leverage these donations and maximize their effect.

CHARITABLE TRUSTS

Another possible vehicle for long-term planning is the charitable trust, which is an irrevocable trust through which you intend to benefit one or more charities. *Importantly, however, you can also benefit yourself or your heirs through a charitable trust, above and beyond the enormous tax benefits.*

There are two basic kinds of charitable trusts: charitable remainder trusts and charitable lead trusts. Both offer incredible tax advantages, as well as asset protection against predatory lawsuits.

The Charitable Remainder Trust (CRT)

A charitable remainder trust is a great strategy for people who want to live on the assets of a trust, benefit from charitable tax breaks, and then leave whatever remains to charity when they pass away. Candidates include older people who worry about how much to give away each year without running short. CRTs are also especially useful for businesspeople who have concentrated positions in things such as properties, single stocks, or a company. It can help you support your favorite charities, diversify your holdings, *and* save a lot of taxes in the bargain.

Let's suppose Doug owns an investment property that he bought many years ago for $200,000. It's now worth $800,000. If he sells his investment property outright, he will need to pay a capital gains tax of the amount ($800,000 − $200,000) × 20% = $120,000.

Instead, Doug can set up a CRT and place the property in it before the sale. Now when Doug sells the property, the sale is exempt from capital gains, and Doug has saved $120,000.

"Fine," you may say, "but what if Doug doesn't want to give all that money to charity?" *With a CRT, he doesn't have to.* Each year, he can take out some of the money from a CRT for his personal use. Let's see how that works.

CRAT or CRUT

Charitable remainder trusts are irrevocable trusts that divide into two interesting flavors: CRAT (charitable remainder annuity trust) and CRUT (charitable remainder unitrust).

In a CRAT, Doug can pay himself (or a designated beneficiary) a fixed *annuity amount* every year. In a CRUT, Doug can pay himself (or a designated beneficiary) a fixed *percentage of the balance of funds* remaining in the trust each year.

We can't cover all the details here, but the bottom line is that Doug can take out between 5 and 50 percent of his *initial* contribution value every year in a CRAT, or he can take out between 5 and 50 percent of the *remainder* value in a CRUT every year.

Either way, a charitable remainder trust is a wonderful thing.

Just Remember that the IRS Is Not Stupid

You may ask, "Hey, what if I just put the property in the

CRT, sell it, and then take the money out in two years (50 percent each year) and just leave $1 for charities?"

The IRS is not stupid, so a few added rules make sure a decent cut ultimately goes for charitable purposes. Actuarially speaking, 10 percent of the initial contribution value must go to charities in the end, and the odds of the trust value going to zero must be less than 5 percent.

In the case of Doug, of his original $800,000 in property value, a minimum of $80,000 must eventually go to charities. The rest he really can take out for his personal use. The $80,000 that goes to charities is tax deductible right away, so for a person in the top combined marginal tax rate of 50 percent, the income tax savings is another $40,000.

In the final analysis, Doug gives $80,000 to charities he cares about but saves $160,000 in taxes. Moneywise, he is $80,000 ahead.

The Charitable Lead Trust

A charitable lead trust (CLT) is the exact inverse of the charitable remainder trust and serves a very different purpose. In a CLT, the income produced by the trust goes to charities now, but when the grantor dies, the remainder of the trust goes to his or her heirs. The grantor cannot derive income from the trust. It's all about supporting charities now and heirs later.

A CLT can be structured in a variety of ways to provide significant tax advantages for both grantor and eventual beneficiaries.

THE PRIVATE FOUNDATION

The creation of a private charitable foundation will be appropriate for only the superwealthy—people with upward of $50 million in assets. It operates as an independent nonprofit in much the same way a company operates with a board, officers, and paid staff.

Unlike some other vehicles, your private foundation has few restrictions in its fund-raising and giving. Most importantly, it can raise money from others and give it away to individuals, to foreign charitable causes, and to other places often unavailable for tax-deductable donations. On the downside, the costs and hassle are as high as running any corporation: you must complete all the strict bookkeeping required of a corporation, and your foundation will be subject to IRS audits.

Despite the effort, a private foundation can have enormous tax benefits for the extremely wealthy. If Warren

Buffett turns $1 million into $1 billion, he faces a gigantic tax burden. But by donating that money to Bill Gates's foundation or to his own foundation, he can avoid pretty much all the related taxes.

Just as importantly, a private foundation can endure well beyond your own lifetime, administered by your family or others you trust. If you have the means, it's the ideal way to support a cause you believe in.

PILLAR 6: EXIT PLANNING

Whether or not you ever plan to exit your business, you should plan as if you intend to exit soon. This may sound like extreme advice, but it actually represents simple prudence. Planning for an exit means separating your "self" from your "business," hiring the right management, and creating all the formal structures to enable the business to run without you.

In short, if you're not making yourself expendable, all you have is a job, not a sellable business.

It takes much time and much thought to plan your own expendability. Usually, the planning and preparation take years. If you just get up one day and say, "I think I'll put my company out for sale next week," you will likely create a catastrophe.

HURDLES FOR LIFESTYLE ENTREPRENEURS

Lifestyle entrepreneurs usually love their work, so they rarely think about an exit. That means they face special hurdles when the moment inevitably arrives.

Often, they have mixed their personal and business finances, making it difficult for someone to cleanly buy them out. Many times, they have also hired family members who would suffer under another boss—or their employees have become like family, and they don't want them harmed in a merger or buyout.

In addition, lifestyle entrepreneurs often fail to create a formal management structure that can survive their own departure. This includes a serious lack of delegation. Often, the lifestyle entrepreneur—be it a doctor, a landscape gardener, a building contractor, a CPA, a lawyer, or an art dealer—is doing half the company work, handling the books, and doing most of the sales.

These folks are neck-deep in the day-to-day and unable to see the company as separate from themselves. Anyone wishing to buy it will have an equally hard time seeing how it can be run after the founder is gone.

ARE YOU QUALIFIED TO SELL YOUR OWN BUSINESS?

If you wanted to sell off your business tomorrow, do you have any idea of how you would price it?

Take my friend Al, who runs a small, successful government contracting business. One year, the market was very favorable, and people were paying top multiples for such companies—a multiple being the acquisition price as a multiple of annual earnings. Al decided to sell. To save money, however, he decided to do the deal all on his own.

How should he price his business? He looked at the multiples of publicly traded government contracting companies—the public price-to-earnings, or PE, ratio. The PEs of public companies often run way above ten and can run close to twenty, so he set his price at twenty times his annual earnings.

Result? No offers.

A year later, the market turned south, and the best time to sell a government contracting business passed. At last, Al got a professional business appraiser involved who priced his business at only about three-and-a-half times earnings. At the height of the market, said the professional, my friend might have received seven times earnings, but that's all. He wasn't a public company and couldn't expect anything close to ten or twenty times.

HURDLES FOR ENTERPRISE ENTREPRENEURS

Enterprise entrepreneurs usually start a business with a clear idea that one day they will exit and realize as much equity as they can when they go. That means they've probably created the necessary management structures and cleanly separated their personal finances.

Often, however, enterprise entrepreneurs are so overconfident about their exit payout that they have failed to create wealth *beyond* their business, and they have not done significant personal financial planning around the long-term opportunities and consequences of their exit.

They have not looked *beyond* their last day at the company.

YOU CAN'T DO THIS ALONE

Let me start your process by saying that you should never plan your exit with only you as your advisor. That's because knowing your business and knowing how to sell your business are two entirely different things.

You actually need a small team to sell a business properly, and you should think about this group as the presale advisors, the deal team, and the postsale squad. The chart that follows appears courtesy of the highly recommended book *Cash Out Move On* by John H. Brown. You may not need all the people in the chart, but you should certainly figure out where you will obtain each kind of expertise.

Advisor	Pre-Sale	The Sale	Post-Sale
Certified Public Assistant	X	X	X
Exit Planning Advisor	X	X	X
Business/Tax Attorney	X		
Estate Planning Attorney	X		X
M&A Attorney		X	
Business Consultant	X	X	
Financial Advisor	X	X	X
Transaction Intermediary (Investment Banker/Business Broker)		X	
Business Appraiser	X		

Source: *Cash Out Move On*, by John H. Brown

THE FOUR BASIC EXIT STRATEGIES

There are four basic ways to exit a business. I present them in a hierarchy, with the most valuable option first. By "most valuable," I mean most likely to create a good amount of liquidity from your equity in a company. Not included in the four basic methods is the rare event of an initial public offering, which may generate great liquidity but is not fundamentally an exit strategy for the entrepreneur.

The first two strategies involve a purchase by an outside company. Such a purchase might be called a *merger* or an *acquisition.* Don't be confused by these terms: the difference is entirely in the size of the acquirer. If a larger company acquires a smaller one, that is considered an acquisition. If they are of more or less equal size, it's a merger. In the end, it's all the same from your point of view.

I. SELLING TO A STRATEGIC BUYER

For most businesses, selling to a strategic buyer offers the best exit option and realizes the most equity for the owners. That's because the business offers some important strategic value to the purchaser, which is usually another company in a related field.

A strategic buyer buys a business for reasons beyond its cash flow. Hence, they pay a premium. *Importantly, that strategic value will almost always be limited to a very small window of time.*

One of my clients owns a sizable emergency medical practice that covers most of a northeastern state. He contracts with local hospitals to provide emergency services, and he's done very well. As of this writing, a much bigger national group has expressed an interest in acquiring his business because it covers the whole country with the exception of a few states, including his. Acquiring my client's business would help close that gap.

That company has a reason to buy that goes above and beyond financial reasons, so it is likely to pay the highest value. *At least during a strategic window of opportunity.*

Another example would be a corollary business that sees a way to expand its relationship with an existing client base. The same clients may use two different, related services that can be combined. An example of this kind of strategic buy would be Facebook's acquisition of WhatsApp. This acquisition expanded Facebook's relationship with its clients and simultaneously eliminated a potential competitor. WhatsApp was losing money at the time, so its value was *entirely* strategic.

2. SELLING TO A FINANCIAL BUYER

Strategic buyers are rare. Ninety percent of external buyers are *financial buyers*, especially of small- to medium-sized firms. Small to medium firms tend to have less strategic value, and the sales price is derived purely from the revenue the business has proven to generate in the past.

Well, *mostly* it's all about earnings, but some strategy may come into play. For example, financial buyers may be performing a roll-up operation in which they purchase several smaller businesses, package them into a bigger business, and then sell to get a higher multiple. In the marketplace, a larger business tends to have a higher multiple than a smaller company.

Sometimes a savvy financial buyer will perform a *leveraged buyout.* In essence, they take out a loan to buy the cash flow of a company with substantial revenue—hence the term "leverage." Because interest payments are tax deductible while dividends are not, they create value by extracting tax savings.

Sophisticated financial buyers from private equity firms may want to bring in professional management after the sale, particularly if they are buying what was a lifestyle business run by someone without a business background.

Often, however, the original owner will be required to stay on for a certain time to run the business, if only to help with the transition.

Making a Clean Exit after an External Sale

Unfortunately, original owners usually have a poor experience when they stay on after a buyout.

Take my client Davis, a math professor who wrote a highly sophisticated book about properly valuing businesses and investments. Thanks to this successful book, Davis began a consulting company and launched a software product to aid people doing valuations. Eventually, his company was acquired by a major financial institution, which asked him to stay on as co-CEO with someone they'd appoint.

Sound like a dream come true? Read on.

Soon after the initial sale, the big financial institution was itself acquired by an even bigger institution. Davis liked the first co-CEO but felt that the new co-CEO was an idiot. Naturally, he hated sharing power and decision making with this person. His original employees had no respect for the new co-CEO or for the financial institution itself, and they started underperforming or heading out the door.

Things started heading south.

Sadly, as part of the sale, Davis had agreed to stay on for five full years as co-CEO. On top of that, he also signed a noncompete agreement for an additional two years after his departure. In theory, Davis was stuck for seven tedious years. But after just two years he couldn't stand it and quit—respecting the noncompete agreement and doing pretty much nothing in the way of work for the next five years, except a bit of lecturing.

Recently, when the noncompete finally expired, Davis

started a new consulting business in the same arena. You will be glad to know that it's doing quite well. He has told me his two younger partners are eager to realize their equity and sell out, but Davis is resisting. He says he's "been there, done that" and would just like to keep operating his new business forever.

Davis's tale is not at all unusual. In fact, based on my many conversations with entrepreneurs, both as clients and as friends, I would say his story is more the rule than the exception. People who have run their own businesses rarely find happiness working for others, and the experience of seeing someone else make bad decisions about your baby can be excruciating.

The lesson? Think twice before selling something you love. If you do sell, make it a clean break. It may even be worth taking less money up front in order to enable that departure.

3. MAKING AN INTERNAL SALE TO EMPLOYEES

Sometimes it's not feasible to find external buyers because of either market reasons or internal reasons. In this case, an entrepreneur may turn to internal buyers—key employees who could eventually run the business on their own.

Most of the time, however, these employees do not have

access to significant capital, so they earn their ownership through working harder and taking lower pay over an extended period. Alternatively, the business can take out a loan to buy out the original entrepreneurs, with the loan becoming the liability of the new employee-owners.

Either way, an internal sale is a long process fraught with risk and uncertainty. Only rarely does it generate the same value as an external sale.

Internal buyouts are common in physicians' private practices. An older doctor will take on a younger partner, and then, over a period of perhaps ten years, the younger doctor becomes the primary owner of the business by paying off the older. The loyalties of patients are, in theory, gradually transferred, and little by little, the older doctor fades out.

The same arrangement may appear to be the only alternative in many lifestyle businesses, especially when the founder has key connections to clients and suppliers that can only be transferred over time, along with the equity.

The pitfalls, however, are many. You could intend to sell the business to one employee, and then that employee might get sick or lose interest. The business could go south during the buyout period. The loyalties of key clients may not transfer so readily. The parties to the deal may become angry at one another, years into the deal. The list goes on.

Consider an ESOP

An employee stock ownership plan, or ESOP, can overcome some of the difficulties of an internal sale because *all* employees become the buyers through their retirement funds. It's an increasingly popular alternative to the traditional internal buyout.

In an ESOP, you set up a retirement trust that buys your shares in the company over time. Contributions to the trust can be made by employees as part of their retirement contributions or by the company. These contributions are tax deductible. The trust can even borrow money from the bank to buy shares from you, with the loan being paid back by company distributions to the trust. Eventually, the trust owns the company.

Put another way, in a normal retirement plan, company and employee contributions are used to buy stocks and bonds. In an ESOP, they are used to buy out the owners.

The shares in the ESOP trust are then earmarked for individual employees through vesting. Usually, you will include all full-time employees over twenty-one, and the earmarks are made according to a formula, usually based on seniority. Vesting may take many years. When employees leave, the company must buy back their stock.

When the transaction is complete, employees will own shares of the business through their qualified retirement plans. *In other words, the employees will have bought out the entrepreneur with pretax dollars.* Because of this substantial tax advantage, the entrepreneur usually gets a far better exit valuation than through a simple internal buyout.

ESOPs are complex, and you certainly need an expert to advise you on how to do one properly, but basically, you are setting up a kind of private marketplace in which you can receive liquidity for your own equity—even while retaining company control. You are also providing for the retirement of your employees and giving them added motivation and a reason to stay.

Thanks to the special tax rules governing ESOPs, you can sometimes receive a valuation even greater than a sale to an outside buyer.

Perhaps most importantly, with an ESOP you are not depending on any particular individual to perform.

4. PASSING THE BUSINESS TO CHILDREN

Many lifestyle entrepreneurs dream of passing their businesses on to their children. Most see this dream dashed.

As dreams go, passing on the business does seem natural. The successful lifestyle entrepreneur loves their work, knows it can generate a good cash flow, and hopes their children will carry on the family tradition—even as they themselves retire into the background. Not only does this paint a lovely picture, but for many, the alternative of passing their work and their income to strangers also seems fraught with pain.

Unfortunately, when we look at the hierarchy of exit strategies, attempting to pass your business on to your children almost always represents the very lowest value return to yourself, along with the highest probability of failure.

For starters, it's unlikely you will realize *any* of your equity in the transfer of ownership itself. Are your children prepared to buy you out for the value you could receive from others? More likely, you will simply "pass it on" with no nest egg created for your retirement.

The likelihood of the business itself failing is also very high. Rarely are the kids as interested in the business or as committed as the parent, so they simply do not work as hard.

If the entrepreneur was counting on a cash flow generated by the business to fund their retirement, then the failure of the business could catastrophically ruin that retirement.

Then there's the inevitable enmity that arises between siblings, as well as between the inheriting child—or worse, children—and parent. The complexities and opportunities for conflict are manifold. One need only recall the plot of Shakespeare's play *King Lear*. Lear decides to retire as king and divide up his kingdom among his three daughters while granting himself a nice retirement. As a result, everything goes to hell, and fast.

If you decide, against all odds, to pursue the Lear route, do it in concert with highly qualified tax and estate attorneys. Indeed, in the case of family arrangements, outside experts are especially crucial.

Consider a Nonqualified Retirement Plan

To better ensure your retirement income in a family succession, you should consider a formal vehicle such as a nonqualified deferred compensation plan, which puts formal obligations on the firm to fund a certain lifestyle for the retiring entrepreneur.

That way, assets to fund your retirement are separated from

other business assets and become eligible for tax deferral benefits. The plan is "nonqualified" under the ERISA laws because it is not offered to all employees. Unfortunately, unlike a qualified plan, the funds could run the risk of forfeiture in the event of a bankruptcy.

ALWAYS PREPARE FOR AN *OPTIONAL EXIT*

I have said that every entrepreneur should always be preparing for an exit. But I did not mean to imply that an exit is mandatory or always a good idea. What I really should have said is, "Don't box yourself *in* to the business or *out* of the business." In other words, "Always be preparing for an optional exit." Delegate. Create structures. Separate out your finances. Make yourself redundant. *Only then* decide whether and when to go.

As in most of life, timing is everything. The window of opportunity for a good sale may close. At the last minute, you may not be able to bear the loss of control, satisfaction, structure, relationship, or community inherent in your business. As the deal evolves, you may see you could only sell by agreeing to become an employee for a specific period—a status that may make you miserable.

Even an enterprise entrepreneur, who may have begun a business with the sole goal of eventually selling his or her stake, should consider carefully before actually walking out the door. *What is it you will do that you cannot do now? Spend a year circling the globe? Then what?*

Your business may well form the core of your life. Without it, you may have a hard time creating a life that ensures both *meaning* and *purpose*. In chapter 5, we'll look more deeply into those two words as they apply to entrepreneurs. For now, let's just say they don't necessarily imply a full exit later in life.

Indeed, taking the steps to ensure your business can successfully run itself without your day-to-day touch means that you are preparing for what may be the modern ideal, a work-optional lifestyle. Such a lifestyle means that maybe you *can* go flying around the world or play golf three days a week but still drop in from time to time to make sure the business is ticking over the way you like.

A work-optional lifestyle means that you have control over your own fate, with the ongoing freedom to sell or not to sell. And of course, *when the time is right*, to sell for the best possible price.

CHAPTER 3

The Process of Wealth Management

The problem with most financial planning lies in the very concept of a "plan."

Usually, when you engage a financial planner, you will write a check for $3,000 or $4,000 minimum, turn over a list of your assets and expenses, attend a couple of meetings, and then get back a highly detailed plan. This plan represents the deliverable from the engagement, and everyone feels as if they've done their job.

Your financial plan will be beautifully presented—probably in a thick, embossed binder. And it will have been generated by a piece of software designed to spew out many, many pages of charts and graphs, including a whole chapter of disclaimers.

Most often, this plan proves not only difficult to read but also nearly impossible to carry out. Why? Not just because the approach was generic and cookie-cutter but, more importantly, because planning is not a one-time event.

Financial well-being is not achieved through a one-time plan, no matter how detailed and filled with charts. *Financial well-being is achieved by a rigorous, repeatable process practiced over many years.*

Within a few short weeks after the computer spews out those many pages, something in every entrepreneur's situation will change. Within a few months, the original plan usually becomes just one more binder gathering dust on your office shelf—a binder that you do not read.

Only a *process* works over time.

THE GOALS OF A GOOD PROCESS

In chapter 2, we learned about the six pillars of wealth management. Now you need to understand the full *process* of wealth management, beginning with the realization that it involves more than just good investing.

You also need to understand the proper role of a financial advisor.

My own process for wealth management was developed through my participation in a remarkable roundtable of financial advisors—a roundtable that grew out of a workshop given by John Bowen. Bowen built two financial advisory firms; one reached $1.5 billion of assets under management, and the other $25 billion. He achieved that feat by keeping a laser focus on repeatable, long-term *processes*.

The overall goal of my own process is to relieve entrepreneurs of the drudgery of keeping their personal finances in good order. It recognizes that you will never have time to fully develop your own expertise in finance—that you have a hard enough time running your business, keeping up with the changes in your industry, and building your personal and business relationships.

Not everyone needs a highly involved financial advisor with this kind of process in place. But I'm pretty sure you, as an entrepreneur, do. In this chapter, I lay out my personal process as a model for the process of working with *any* financial advisor.

INFORMATION AT ALL TIMES

My own wealth management process has been designed to understand an entrepreneur's financial picture not at one point in time but all the time. It's a method for ensuring that a financial advisor stays on top of the client's situation month in and month out. Only with this kind of total understanding can an advisor provide the best advice and solutions within the ever-changing circumstances of modern financial life.

In other words, a good advisor and a good client both recognize that planning rests on two constants: *change and the awareness of change.* Awareness, of course, must go in both directions. Advisors like me do more than advise; we act on behalf of our clients. A good process must ensure that a client knows what the advisor is doing, when it's happening, and why.

Too often, clients do not understand or do not even know what their financial advisors, wealth managers, or investment brokers are up to with their money. With my process, I ensure that decisions are not just understood by my clients but that we stay on the same page as well.

Another information loop involves outside domain experts. No financial advisor has complete expertise in all aspects of wealth management—the six pillars we discussed in chapter 2.

It's simply impossible for any one person to gather the necessary knowledge in each of these areas and keep that knowledge up to date. In fact, most advisors have deep expertise in only one of the six pillars. My specialty, for example, is investments. I do not pretend to know enough about estate planning, tax law, or exit planning to fully advise my clients in these areas.

My process ensures that outside experts with supporting solutions are engaged when needed, and I monitor my clients' situations through a disciplined, ongoing information cycle.

ADVISORS VERSUS MANAGERS

As we explore the proper role of a financial advisor, I should issue a warning about the titles or "hats" that people in my profession wear: *advisor, planner, manager, agent,* or *broker.*

Usually (but not always), people who call themselves "financial planners" do not manage assets on behalf of their clients. They tend to do planning and charge a one-time or hourly fee. They may be a Registered Investment Advisor (RIA), or they may not be.

Financial advisors or wealth managers may manage their clients' assets and make investments on their behalf. If they are brokers, the assets are usually held in the brokerage firm that employs them. If they are independent RIAs, the assets are usually held by a third-party custodian.

People who call themselves "wealth managers" tend to work with wealthier clients. Financial advisors tend to work across a broader range of incomes. But you will find no hard-and-fast rules. Let me emphasize that such hats may be worn or removed at will.

For the sake of convenience, I will refer to everyone who both advises and acts on behalf of their clients as "financial advisors." Just remember that you cannot be certain of anyone's precise role or way of doing business just from their title. You need to ask.

In chapter 5, we will talk about how to choose a financial advisor, regardless of the hat he or she chooses to wear.

CUSTODY OF ASSETS

No doubt you noticed the important difference in the previous discussion between advisors who *hold* the assets of their clients and those merely *authorized to manage* those assets. The common word is *custody*, but the definition of that word remains unclear. An advisor may have *custody* whether the advisor actually holds the assets or not.

In my case, I have the authority to make investment decisions on behalf of my clients and to charge them a fee deducted from their assets. However, my clients' assets are not held by me directly; they are held by Fidelity Investments, an independent firm. I feel strongly that this is the proper arrangement between a client and a financial advisor, because it goes a long way toward preventing criminal activity.

The infamous Bernie Madoff both held the assets of his clients *and* made their investment decisions. That allowed him to keep two sets of books—one to show his clients and one to steal their money. Such a scam would have been impossible if a reputable third party had held the assets.

The overall message? Inquire closely about the specific custodial arrangements made by any financial advisor, regardless of his or her title or institutional affiliation, and choose an advisor who uses a third-party custodian with a solid reputation. The top two custodians in the United States are presently Charles Schwab and Fidelity Investments.

This advice may vary if you consider an in-house advisor at a large full-service brokerage such as Merrill Lynch or Wells Fargo. You may perhaps elect to place your confidence in such an institution, even though it is acting as both your custodian and your broker, and even though its own motives may be mixed.

However, if you work with an *independent advisor*, make

sure he or she is not both investing your money and holding it in his or her own accounts.

THE DISCOVERY MEETING

The process of wealth management begins with a carefully structured series of meetings with a prospective client, launched with the *discovery meeting.*

I need to discover the client, and the client needs to discover me. At this meeting, I ask a large number of questions, including philosophical inquiries such as "What does money mean to you?"

I really do need to understand an entrepreneur's life goals, short and long term, if I am to help him or her reach those goals. I need to understand income and expenses, assets and liabilities, aspirations, interests, and hobbies. Many people are supporting their parents, disabled siblings, children with special needs, or children with drug problems. They're paying alimony or considering a speculation in a new business. I will delve into a potential client's community engagement, charitable inclinations, church attendance—*everything.*

I ask about everything because without understanding everything, I cannot really grasp a client's overall financial picture. Money really does touch every aspect of life.

In general, I break out my questions into these categories:

1. Values: How do you see money? What do you hope to accomplish with money?
2. Goals: Long term, short term, personal, family, social, global
3. Relationships
4. Assets, liabilities, income, expenses, lifestyle, lifestyle aspirations
5. Interests and hobbies
6. Other advisors the client may be working with: Are these advisors reactive or proactive? What is their process?

Of course, I also encourage my prospective clients to ask *me* a lot of questions about my own past, my own goals, and my approach to financial management. Because we are heading into a long-term process together, not into a one-time plan, the quality of our relationship will matter a great deal. We must get a gut feeling about each other.

Usually, by the end of such a meeting, I know whether I can provide substantial value to a prospective client, and I will only go to the next step if I think I can provide that value. If not, I will point them to other advisors or simply ask them to read certain books. The prospective client must also, of course, decide whether they can work with me. Even more, *will they enjoy working with me in a trusting relationship?* If both sides decide to continue the exploration of the process and the relationship, we will move on to the next meeting.

RED FLAGS

Just about all financial advisors hold discovery meetings, although few go into sufficient depth with their prospective clients. We'll get to the questions you should ask at such a meeting in the next chapter, but here are some red flags to watch out for.

The first red flag should be raised if a financial advisor tries to sell you a specific product at that first meeting, such as an annuity, an insurance plan, or a fund. It's way too soon for such a pitch to occur, and that should tell you that the "advisor" is really a salesperson.

The second red flag should be raised if the advisor does not clarify the way in which they would take custody of your investments and the way in which they would report back to you or track your assets.

The third red flag should go up if your advisor seems to be too much of a lone wolf, working without outside experts. If someone pretends to have a deep understanding of tax law *and* investment strategy *and* estate planning, something is wrong.

In my own discovery meetings, I always spend a little time explaining the ecosystem of financial advising. If clients don't go with me, I want to make sure they don't make the grave mistake of falling into the hands of someone who does not have their best interests at heart.

In the following chart, you will see an overview of the general process that should follow a discovery meeting with any good financial advisor.

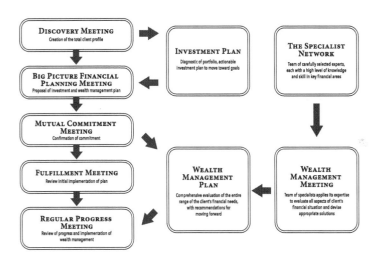

THE SECOND MEETING: BIG-PICTURE FINANCIAL PLAN

If an entrepreneur wishes to move forward, and I think it's a good fit, I will go off after that first meeting and put together a big-picture plan to discuss at the *proposal meeting.*

It's a very simple plan, running about three pages, based on the six pillars of wealth management.

The first page gives a brief summary of the entrepreneur's situation as I understand it: monetary philosophy, goals, relationships, business interests, assets, liabilities, expenses, personal interests, hobbies, social engagement, charitable inclinations, and so forth.

The second page offers a high-level investment strategy based on the summary on page one. Here, I lay out how much income I think the entrepreneur needs now and will need for retirement—along with supporting kids in school and paying off liabilities.

The investment strategy truly fits on one page. If you remember my dictum that a good investment strategy is simple but hard to carry out, you will understand why.

The third page presents a wealth management action plan— the process of moving forward. Here, I include gaps I have seen in the client's financial life that must be addressed. One entrepreneur may be doing their own taxes each year and missing a lot of deductions. Another will have young children but has yet to do any planning on their behalf in case of his or her own death or incapacity.

In other words, this third page addresses each of the six pillars that will require expert help and will demand a long-term management process for the individual client. The expertise for each pillar will be found by me, as I act like a primary care physician, calling in specialists from my network as needed: a CPA, an estate attorney, a business exit expert—whoever is needed.

I present my very short, three-page proposal at the second meeting. Entrepreneurs who have been handed thick binders by financial advisors in the past may be shocked, but most are relieved to see something immediately comprehensible and free of filler.

We go over the entrepreneur's feedback on the plan and see what needs to be adjusted. Then we size up our potential engagement together and discuss whether we want to move forward together. If your prospective financial advisor hands you a thick binder, ask him or her to summarize each section with simple words, and look at the underlying process and investment philosophy rather than the charts.

Sometimes a potential client will become very excited and want to sign up with me on the spot. But I don't want anyone to make a decision at this second meeting. I tell potential clients that such a decision involves a long-term relationship and that it is too important for any quick judgments. I tell them to sit on the proposal for a week or so and come back for a third meeting.

THE THIRD MEETING: COMMITMENT

Like many advisors, I call the third meeting a *mutual commitment meeting*. Some call it the onboarding meeting.

The cool-down period has passed. The plan has been adjusted based on feedback from the second meeting. Papers have been prepared for an advisory agreement, which gives me authority to manage assets through a third-party custodian. The client will also sign papers with that third-party custodian—in my case, Fidelity Investments—so that it will begin holding his or her assets.

If everything's a go, the entrepreneur has become a client.

THE FOURTH MEETING: FULFILLMENT

The fourth meeting, often called the *fulfillment meeting*, comes anywhere from two to four weeks later. At this point, I have begun moving the new client's money into the hands of my third-party custodian, and a number of investments will have been placed.

Now I need to sit down with the entrepreneur to explain what I have been up to and how the process is moving forward.

It's not unusual to encounter a little nervousness at this point, maybe even some buyer's remorse. In spite of all our conversations, a client may have woken up one morning and suddenly realized, "Hey, this guy is moving my money around. What's going on? Am I crazy to do this?"

Clients may have already received the first statements from the third-party custodian (again, in my case, Fidelity), and I need to teach them how to read those statements. At this point, I usually do provide a binder, but it's intended for keeping statements and other financial records properly organized. I ask the client to use that binder for everything and to make notes there with questions for our future meetings.

This fourth meeting always proves important and timely. It firmly establishes our working relationship, and it brings the entrepreneur fully into the loop.

REGULAR PROGRESS MEETINGS

After that important fourth meeting, I meet with my clients a minimum of once a quarter—more often, of course, if their situation is complex.

At these regular meetings, I will first report on what we have accomplished against the six pillars in the previous quarter with an emphasis on investments. And then I will make sure I find out what has changed in the client's situation.

Life moves fast, and often I learn of previously unreported changes in a client's situation that require some action on my part—whether it be a new opportunity, a new goal, a new responsibility, or a potential danger.

Finally, we go back to my wealth management action plan, the third page of that three-page plan, and we decide on our priorities for the coming quarter.

Aside from the ongoing investment or wealth preservation pillar, I try to focus actions on just one pillar per quarter so that I do not overwhelm my client with actions and changes. Over the next quarter, we may focus on tax mitigation; in the next, we may work on charitable planning; in the next, on heir protection; and so forth.

The regular progress meetings are the first repeatable loop in an iterative process.

BRINGING IN THE DOMAIN EXPERTS

After each regular progress meeting, I take the information I have gathered and loop in my domain experts. As I mentioned, these may include CPAs, attorneys, bankers, insurance experts, practice advisors, and other specialists. I will call a meeting with four or five of these people, sit down, and review the client's situation, including all the updates.

At these meetings, I'm looking for expert advice, forward actions, and warnings.

An attorney might say, "Wow, this entrepreneur really needs to add such and such clause to his estate plan." The CPA might say, "She's not deducting a major expense, and she really needs to bring that into her accounting now so she can claim that deduction on April 15."

Such experts see things I would not see, and they bring invaluable opinions and ideas to the big picture of the client's overall wealth—the picture that I must have as the "primary care physician" managing my client's financial health.

I will then bring these ideas and warnings to my client so that we can take action together. It's up to the client whether to use my recommended CPA, attorney, or other expert to implement these actions. They may choose to use their own expert or to do the work themselves. There's no obligation, but I do want to make sure that the action occurs. I am only authorized to take *independent action* on my clients' investment portfolios.

FOCUS ON THE PROCESS

Both the regular progress meetings and the repeated loop with the experts occur at least every quarter, and together, these two loops form the core of my approach to wealth management—not a single plan but *a relationship and a process*. By engaging in a similar process with a good financial advisor, your financial situation will improve year to year, with far fewer bumps in your fiscal road than you probably experience now.

The process requires discipline, outside expertise, and constant communication.

I compare a sound financial process with regular exercise and a proper diet. A person does not become healthy and strong by going to the gym one time or eating one head of lettuce. A person becomes healthy and strong by going to the gym two or three days a week, every week, for their entire lives and by eating right day in and day out.

Here's a summary of the functions any good financial advisor must serve if he or she is to build the six pillars of your house of wealth:

1. The financial advisor will use a consultative process to establish a close relationship with you in order to gain a detailed understanding of your values, needs, goals, resources, and obligations. No cookie-cutter plans.
2. The advisor will coordinate a team of specialists who offer customized solutions designed to fit your specific needs. This team will take into account a range of interrelated financial services, such as investment management, insurance, tax planning, estate planning, and business succession planning. No lone wolves.
3. The advisor will deliver these customized solutions only in close consultation with you and will work closely with you on an ongoing basis to make sure all gaps and threats in your financial life are identified and addressed proactively. You are always in the loop, and nothing is left out of the loop.

In the next chapter, we'll talk about how to choose and interview an advisor who can help ensure your own financial health.

CHAPTER 4

How to Choose a Financial Advisor

As I have mentioned, the only requirement for becoming a financial advisor is to call yourself a financial advisor. My mother, who is an ob-gyn and knows nothing about money, could call herself a financial advisor, and she would not be breaking any laws.

Generally speaking, however, only three types of people *tend* to call themselves financial advisors. The first step to delegating your wealth management is to understand their roles.

1. Insurance agents: These could be captive agents, working for a single insurance company such as New York Life or MetLife, or they could be independent agents who represent multiple insurance products. In either

case, these folks make their livings earning commissions from the insurance companies. They are under no obligation to disclose how much they make or how they make it. They are the insurance companies' agents; they are not your agents. Still, their business cards may read "financial advisor."

2. Stockbrokers: These folks may work for major Wall Street brokerages such as Goldman Sachs or Morgan Stanley, they may work for banks or other institutions, or they may work as independent broker/dealers. Regardless, their job is to act as the middleman who facilitates transactions. In other words, they earn money when transactions happen. That makes them, at best, intermediaries. At worst, they may be counterparties. In other words, they may actually be working against your interests. How much a stockbroker makes off you is their trade secret. They are certainly not your fiduciary. But their business card may read "financial advisor."

3. Registered Investment Advisors (RIAs): These are the only "financial advisors" who are actually licensed to give financial advice. According to the law as of this writing, insurance agents and stockbrokers are not even allowed to give advice other than what is incidental to the products they sell. RIAs are presently regulated by the Investment Advisors Act of 1940, which requires them to undertake a fiduciary

duty to their clients. By current law, they cannot accept third-party payments. They must also be completely transparent about their conflicts of interest if any exist. I call these pure RIAs to distinguish them from hybrid RIAs, who are RIAs who also have a broker license and/or an insurance license. The latter may even quietly operate these practices as separate companies. One company gives advice and then recommends you to the other company for your investment purchases, receiving both fees and commissions on the same work. I would prefer a hybrid RIA to a broker, but it's best to make sure your financial advisor (or wealth manager) is a pure RIA, not a hybrid RIA. As of now, this at least means he or she is obligated by law to act in your best interest and that conflicts of interest are minimized.

In my experience, I do see a direct relationship between disclosure requirements and honor among financial advisors. In my opinion, fees and kickbacks should be disclosed, and advisors should indeed be required to act in the best interests of their clients.

As it stands, however, the situation is in flux, and you certainly cannot trust regulators to protect you. You need to make yourself personally aware of your advisor's *true* role in the financial world and his or her obligations to your financial well-being.

OVERTRUSTING YOUR BROKER

It's hard to resist storied names such as Merrill Lynch or Morgan Stanley—regardless of the number of times they have appeared in the news for padding their fees or misleading their clients. Like Carlos from the Caribbean, whose story I told in chapter 2, you may think there's some safety in a big name, while the opposite is probably the case.

In hopes of shifting your view, let me tell you one more cautionary tale about stockbrokers, this one from my first book, *Physician Wealth Management Made Easy.*

Dr. Anderson had become a multimillionaire physician with sizable investments, but he had never had much time to choose them wisely. Like Carlos, he depended on a storied Wall Street brokerage. This brokerage paid its senior executives *$4 billion in the same year the firm needed a federal bailout.* During that famous year of 2008, three of Dr. Anderson's accounts lost a great deal of money.

The personal hurdle he faced? Not the big market crash but big-name market scamsters.

One of Dr. Anderson's investments was a US Treasury account, through which his big-name money manager purchased Treasury bills and bonds on his behalf. The year 2008 might have been bad for stocks, but it was a great year for all US Treasury securities. The stock turmoil caused investors to flock to Treasuries, driving prices up 13 percent. Dr. Anderson's Treasury account, however, lost 30 percent.

What could cause a discrepancy like this? Well, his "full-service" brokerage also worked as a primary dealer in the Treasury market.

It bought securities and resold them to its customers at a huge markup, which effectively wiped out all client profits and even put some clients into the negative.

The brokerage made money. Dr. Anderson did not. Hence, the big bonuses to senior executives at the storied Wall Street firm.

In that same year of 2008, the Standard & Poor's (S&P) 500 Index lost 38 percent. However, Dr. Anderson's stock account lost 62 percent. How could that happen? Well, the brokerage performed frequent trades, including extremely high volumes of buys and sells of largely S&P 500 stocks in small lots. His year-end statement had no fewer than 377 pages of transaction records. The sheer volume of trade fees and taxes was devastating to him.

Once again, of course, the brokerage did just fine.

Many Wall Street financial firms like to tell their wealthy clients that they can put their money in investments not available to the general public. Sure enough, like Carlos's family office, Dr. Anderson's broker put nearly 40 percent of his money into a hedge fund.

The good news? To this day, this hedge fund reports that it's "making money." The bad news? These results are not audited or even calculated by a third party.

At last check, the fund was headquartered in Paris, but the Securities and Exchange Commission (SEC) had no record of either the fund or its managers. Could this be another Bernie Madoff-style scam? We still can't be sure. What can we learn from Carlos and Dr. Anderson? *Never hire a Wall Street broker to be your financial advisor. They don't work for you; they work for themselves.*

HOW TO INTERVIEW A FINANCIAL ADVISOR

Even if you reject stockbrokers and find a genuine financial advisor, I have found that shockingly few have made a proper study of investment science. Many are followers of the voodoo theories I discussed in chapter 2. And regardless of their current expertise or commitment, many come from a background in sales. They tend to be highly social, talkative people and may appear "not serious." When confronted with such people, many entrepreneurs end up handling their own finances to their great detriment.

As a businessperson, you need to bring your focus on facts and results to any business discussion, but I urge you to head into an interview with a potential advisor remembering the following truths: (1) you *do* need someone doing this for you, (2) there *are* good people out there doing this, (3) expertise in financial matters *does* exist, (4) you do not have time to build that expertise yourself, and (5) even if you have the expertise, you don't have the time to manage your money the right way.

With that attitude firmly in mind, you should approach the interview of a financial advisor as you would any employee. Because this will be a long-term relationship, everything counts. Make the interview formal and comprehensive. Here's a breakdown of the areas you should consider. I call them the five Cs.

CHARACTER

Make sure your financial advisor offers the highest level of integrity. That means he or she has not entered this profession just to make money but has a higher calling to help people. Often, this can be revealed simply by asking what brought the advisor to this kind of work. "I really get a rush from the stock market" may not be the best answer.

CHEMISTRY

Make sure you can connect with your financial advisor on an emotional level and that he or she "gets" you. Start out by engaging in a bit of small talk to see whether your conversations flow naturally.

CARING

You need to get the sense that an advisor is genuinely concerned about your well-being. This is best determined by *the questions the advisor asks*, unprompted. Do they try to understand your current financial situation in all its aspects? Do they want to know your goals, dreams, aspirations, fears, and worries? Or do they just want to guide you to their latest offering?

COMPETENCY

You need to ask some tough questions to ensure an advisor is technically capable. This means getting past the impressive charts and graphs you will be shown about past performance with other clients. Ask a few technical questions to see whether he or she can answer them confidently. I suggest some later. Also, pull out chapter 2 of this book and see whether they can discuss all of my six pillars of wealth management with some confidence.

During the interview, you will get a sense of the educational level achieved by the advisor. You may even want to inquire about that level. There are people out there acting as financial advisors who did not even complete high school.

COST EFFECTIVENESS

Make sure the advisor delivers true value relative to cost. Most charge 1 percent on assets under management (AUM), and fees should not deviate too greatly from that. Some will offer discounts on larger portfolios. For example, an advisor may charge 1 percent on the first million in assets, and then perhaps 0.7 percent on assets above $1 million up to $5 million and 0.4 percent on everything beyond $5 million.

Remember, however, that brokers and insurance agents receive additional kickbacks from fund companies. If they sell you a mutual fund or an insurance policy, the net cost to you may well double.

Be Especially Wary of Insurance Agents

On investments wrapped in insurance policies, your "advisor" will be getting 3 percent or 3.5 percent above and beyond what they are charging you for advice. Not only does this represent a conflict of interest in their choice of investment vehicle, but you are also absolutely paying fees you should not pay.

That means that over ten years, you can easily give up 35 percent of your wealth without even knowing it.

Truly, if you use an insurance agent as your investment advisor, it is very unlikely you can retire well, because most of your wealth will have been transferred to the insurance company by the time you retire. Not surprisingly, as the least regulated industry in finance, insurance extracts the most money.

A broker is a little better but not much. With a Wall Street broker, you will be paying about 2.5 percent, or losing 25 percent over ten years.

SUGGESTED INTERVIEW QUESTIONS

Here are some suggested questions to ask a potential financial advisor. I am certain you will find the answers revealing. The questions are intentionally similar to questions an employer would ask a potential employee.

1. *Do you have a Series 7 license?* The correct answer is no. A Series 7 license is a broker license. Having this license means your advisor is actually a broker who can take third-party kickbacks without your knowledge.

2. *Do you have license to sell insurance policies?* Again, the correct answer is no. You want a pure RIA as your financial advisor, not an insurance agent.

3. *What license do you have?* The correct answer is Series 65. This is the RIA license that currently requires the holder to act as a fiduciary.

4. *How and when did you become a financial advisor? What brought you to the wealth management business?* Here, you are looking for character: an honest desire to help people.

5. *Tell me your proudest moment as a financial advisor.* Again, you are looking for character.

6. *I'm sure you do great work, but every road has bumps. Tell me about a moment in your work as a financial advisor that made you ashamed.* This question can reveal a great deal—even if the advisor avoids answering it.

7. *What do you enjoy most as a financial advisor?* You must

judge for yourself whether this answer resonates with you.

8. *Who are your clients? Do you work with any particular niche or type of client?* Ideally, the advisor will have extensive and specific experience with entrepreneurs, but don't prompt for this.

9. *Have you heard of Eugene Fama?* If the advisor has not heard of Eugene Fama, Nobel Prize winner and the father of modern finance, you should be very concerned. This single question may be enough to reveal an advisor's knowledge base.

10. *What is your investment philosophy?* Compare this against the brief summary I presented in chapter 2. If an advisor cannot articulate a substantially similar philosophy, look elsewhere.

11. *Who is on your team? What are the resources you rely on to do your job?* You must be sure that your advisor is not operating alone and maintains a significant network of internal or external expertise. Again, don't prompt for the answer. Don't ask, "Do you pull in estate attorneys as needed?"

12. *Tell me about your overall consultative process.* The advisor should be able to lay out a process similar to the one I outlined in chapter 3. Indeed, the advisor should be focused on process and not treat process as an afterthought. If you ask, "How often do we meet?," the advisor should not reply, "As often as you like."

13. *What aspects of wealth management do you help with?* Again, don't prompt with specifics. The advisor should be able to list categories similar to my six pillars.

14. *What are your fees, and how are they structured and billed?* See "Cost Effectiveness" above for a full discussion of proper fees.

15. *Do you personally receive any commissions on transactions?* Remember that these are on top of fees and always represent a conflict of interest.

16. *What do you see as the biggest value you provide to your clients?* This open-ended question should help you understand whether you are working with someone who provides a long-term wealth management process or is simply looking to place your investments and take in a fee.

ARE YOU DEALING WITH A MERE SALESPERSON?

After you have completed this interview, ask yourself, "Is this someone I can trust? Someone who will have my back? Someone I can call in a crisis?"

You don't want to work with a person whose advice will always leave you with a nagging doubt. In the good times, you may not worry about questionable advice or incomplete follow-through. In the good times, you may say to yourself, "Ok, my doubts can be swept under the rug. My portfolio is going up. We have a great time playing golf together." But then, when the rough times come, you will have no one to trust, no one you can rely on to take action.

Once again, all too often, a "financial advisor" is merely a salesperson.

By asking these questions, I hope you can discover the truth behind the business card. But beyond determining competence and trustworthiness, you really do need to find out whether the advisor *cares* about your outcomes. After the interview, ask yourself, "Does this person care? Will this person really try to understand my situation?"

Entrepreneurs often tell me about financial advisors who jumped right to "solutions" barely fifteen minutes into their first conversation. By doing this, such advisors show that they do not really care to understand an entrepreneur's full, often complex situation. They are just trying to push their latest bond offer. Fifteen minutes is not enough to grasp anyone's complete set of financial and personal issues— certainly not those of an active entrepreneur. The "solution" is usually a lucrative product with a high commission that the advisor is eager to close.

If the advisor is just a salesperson, his or her job will essentially be over after the product has been sold. The commission usually comes up front, and these salespeople know that after they gather your assets and score their commission, their time will be better spent on new clients. After that, every phone call with you that does not lead to an additional sale will just be a waste of their time, a cost of doing business. This is especially true of insurance salespeople because brokers can often find ways to churn your stocks and score additional kickbacks on your portfolio.

EDUCATED IN ALL SIX PILLARS

Let me finish this chapter by going back to interview question 13, the one evaluating breadth of knowledge.

Earlier, I said that a good financial advisor cannot possibly offer sufficient expertise in all my six pillars of wealth management. Nevertheless, like a primary care physician who refers you to specialists, he or she must be educated in all six pillars, and a big part of your interview must be an effort to determine their basic knowledge in all six.

I regularly attend training seminars in accounting, law, estate planning, and other areas of concern to my clients. I know I need to pull in genuine expertise as needed, but I make sure I am strong enough in each area that I can identify opportunities and pitfalls in my clients' situations.

HOW DO BIG BROKERAGES TRAIN "ADVISORS"?

Most of the training that "financial advisors" receive at a large brokerage such as Morgan Stanley has little to do with investment strategy and even less to do with wealth management. Most of the training really is in sales. Such institutions will recruit a bunch of young people and give them a list of two hundred numbers to call every day. "Cold-call these numbers and try to schedule an appointment. You're playing a numbers game. The more calls, the more likely you will score. Get used to hearing no and moving on."

Afterward, the office will hold a group meeting and extol the person who made the most calls and scheduled the most meetings.

I experienced this firsthand when I went to a recruiting meeting at a large brokerage, which I found frankly shocking.

By the time such training is over, these "advisors" have become numb to rejection and to people saying no over and over again. Worse, they will have become accustomed to befriending people with the goal of selling them something. They will have learned to take people out for coffee, cultivate their trust, and then move a product. That's their primary skill. And it's how they are evaluated.

At the end of the month, these people are not asked, "Did you help your clients improve their financial situation?" They are asked, "Did you meet your production target? Did you gather enough money from your clients?"

Tax mitigation? Estate planning? Long-term charitable planning? Brokers generally learn little or nothing about such subjects. *Nevertheless, their business cards will often read "financial advisor."*

For example, an entrepreneur may own the buildings in which they operate their business, which makes them commercial real estate investors. As a financial advisor, I need to have enough understanding of commercial real estate tax law to see opportunities for savings and then bring in a CPA with the focused expertise.

My own primary expertise is investing, but another overall financial advisor may have a different primary expertise, such as accounting and tax law. Such an advisor must be sufficiently self-aware to call on outside experts in investing and not try to wing it.

Force yourself to interview more than one potential financial advisor. Make sure they do their homework. Make sure they know their limitations. And please, don't choose a *salesperson*.

CHAPTER 5

Entrepreneur Well-Being

Perhaps you remember the story I began in chapter 1 about the girl I met in college back in China. As you may recall, I started my first business as a tour guide in Tiananmen Square so I could earn the money to take her on vacation to the mountains.

The full tale is inextricably bound with my lifelong entrepreneurial journey and my slow understanding of what I will broadly call *entrepreneur well-being*. I tell this story because every person's true personal wealth goes well beyond their finances, and in this closing chapter, I want you to think about managing your own well-being as closely as your bank account.

I already told you that this girl, who I will call Yu Yang, was beautiful. She was also smart, creative, and capable of great love. After college, in 1989, when I returned to Tiananmen Square not as a profitable tour guide but as a protester during the mass demonstrations for democracy and freedom, I participated in a six-day hunger strike. Yu Yang sat with me every day, risking her own life. I was really touched because, unlike me, she wasn't much interested in democracy and freedom; she just cared about my well-being. Indeed, I said to myself, "If I get through this, I will marry this woman." And so I did.

The day I proposed, I told Yu Yang that I would work hard and become very rich and build her a huge, beautiful house in America.

A couple of years later, I got a scholarship to study mathematics at Carnegie Mellon University in Pittsburgh. At the port of departure, my young wife held my hand and said, "If you see a rainbow in the American sky, that's me missing you."

Two months after I arrived, I got a letter. It had not a single word, just a drawing of a young woman standing at the edge of a vast ocean, her eyes looking longingly into the distance. Behind her was a house—not a big house but a cozy house—with smoke coming out of the chimney.

Behind the house rose a rainbow, and I thought, "What a lucky man I am."

I saved up and eventually brought Yu Yang to America. We both worked hard, not just to survive but to put her through school and someday to enable me to start my own business. For a time, I worked days as a teaching assistant, along with nights as a doorman. She worked as a waitress and attended classes.

Life was hard but full of joy.

But right about then, I had a brilliant idea. The internet had arrived, and anything with a dot-com at the end of it was flying high. If I were to become very rich and build that huge house for my wife, the natural road was through a dot-com. In fact, I was determined to become an actual *billionaire*. Why not? I was smart, the world was brimming with new possibilities, and I was willing to work extremely hard.

I began to create an internet company to facilitate cotton trading on a global scale. To make it happen, I moved to Nashville to talk to farmers, geneticists, cotton traders, and manufacturers so I could find out what made sense in my platform. I also had to fly around talking to venture capitalists. Soon I had a letter of intent from a sizable agribusiness concern and some seed money, and I knew I was on my way.

THE FALL

Yu Yang did not move to Nashville, as she now had a good job in New York. Every two weeks or so, I would fly up for a weekend to see her, but otherwise, we spoke only on the phone. This went on for a solid year, but I was so confident of her love that I did not even consider the possibility that we were drifting apart.

One day, however, I got a call from my beautiful, loyal wife. The one who had stood by my side through hunger strikes and sent me a drawing of a rainbow. She said, "Michael, don't you have a good friend in New Orleans? Instead of coming up this weekend, why don't you go see him? Don't worry about me; I'll be fine."

So I did. I went to New Orleans.

For two days, I tried to call Yu Yang to check in, but she did not answer the phone. A bit worried, I called her best friend.

After a long and awkward pause, the best friend told me, "Michael, I'm so sorry to tell you this, but your wife has met a man in Beijing in an internet chat room. This weekend, she flew to see him."

Pretty much at that same moment, the dot-com bubble burst, and my cotton exchange began to collapse. I was unable to obtain viable clients, and the money dried up.

REALIZATIONS

Suddenly, after having a wonderful wife and an exciting startup, I felt I had nothing. The sword of Damocles had fallen right on my head. At one point, I spent three days just walking along the shoulder of Interstate 65 in Nashville, trying to decide whether to jump into the stream of traffic.

Fortunately, I did not jump onto the freeway, partly because I began to read theories of happiness and understand my all-too-common mistake. I saw that I had been so hell-bent on becoming a billionaire that, like a racehorse, I had put on blinders to stay on the track. *In the expectation that money would someday make me happy, I had actively ignored the actual elements of happiness—love, family, friendships, and so much more.*

In this chapter, I want to tell you what I learned in my research into happiness and into the idea of *well-being* in general. Perhaps it will help you avoid some of the mistakes I made over the years.

Before going any further, however, let me assure you that my story has a happy ending. I later found a much more wonderful woman who has become the true love of my life. As of this writing, we have been married for eleven years, and we have two amazing children. I also found my true calling, not as a cotton trader but as a wealth advisor, and as I have already assured you, ambition will never again distract me from my family.

HAPPINESS AS VITAMIN AND CATALYST

The most important thing to know about happiness is that it is not the result of success. *Indeed, happiness is often the prerequisite for success.*

Common wisdom claims that if you reach a given goal, that achievement will make you happy. If you have a big house, drive a good car, and know you have plenty of cash in the bank, you will be happy. As an entrepreneur, your goalposts may be even higher: build a $100 million business, revolutionize your industry, purchase a private jet.

In other words, you have to do something or own something in order to be happy. Actually, claims the latest research, it's just the other way around: if you are happy, it's much easier to do great things.

Shawn Achor's book *The Happiness Advantage* details this research and has had a deep impact on me.[13] Again and again in the book, successful people have identified their own happiness as a kind of vitamin and catalyst that makes their best efforts possible.

How does happiness help lead to success? When you're happy, you're more attractive to other people. You're more creative. Your mind is more open, you're more observant of what's going on around you, and you draw from those activities more opportunities and resources. In short, happiness opens doors.

An unhappy person constantly dwells on past failures. When you dwell on the past, you can't be open to present opportunities. That's just a fact.[14]

The same studies tell us that the happiness associated with reaching a specific goal is extremely brief. Many have tes-

---

13   Shawn Achor, *The Happiness Advantage: How a Positive Brain Fuels Success in Work and Life* (reprint, Redfern, Australia: Currency Press, 2018).

14   Let me suggest three other great books by Martin Seligman. The first is *Learned Optimism* (New York: Vintage, 2006.) People think they are born with the trait of either optimism or pessimism, but it turns out that optimism can be developed through self-training. The second is *Authentic Happiness: Using the New Positive Psychology to Realize Your Potential for Lasting Fulfillment* (New York: Free Press, 2002). Here he classifies well-being into a hierarchy. On the lowest rung are fleeting pleasures, such as eating an ice cream cone. After pleasure comes joy. But Seligman argues that the highest levels of well-being come from finding meaning and purpose in life. I also recommend Seligman's *Flourish: A Visionary New Understanding of Happiness and Well-Being* (New York: Atria Books, 2012), which furthers his potent ideas.

tified to this great truth, and I have certainly found it to be true for myself. For example, I once bought the luxury car I had always wanted, an Infinity X45. I was thrilled for about two weeks. When I stepped on the gas, the car made a wonderful, adrenaline-producing *whoosh* as it accelerated, and my heartbeat increased.

But alas, after that first couple of weeks, I felt the same when I got behind the wheel as when I drove my old, beat-up Honda. The X45 became just a more expensive form of transportation. I had been happy working all those years to put together the money. The X45 was just a *by-product*, not the *cause*, of my happiness.

YOU CAN LEARN TO BE HAPPY

Now, what if you consider yourself a morose and unhappy person? Perhaps, you even think your unhappiness is genetic.

Again, research shows that in most healthy people, this is simply not true. Indeed, Achor suggests that happiness is our *choice*. We're not born with a certain level of happiness over which we have no control; we can actively make ourselves happy, and *more than 50 percent of happiness comes from our own decision to be happy.*

HAPPINESS REQUIRES A HIGHER MEANING

Of course, the deepest happiness rests on more than your personal well-being. It requires a higher purpose.

Some years after my dot-com debacle, I created a hedge fund in which I found great monetary success. Money came rolling in, but I was alone in my glory. Most days, I never spoke to a soul, not even about money. I simply sat in front of a bank of computer screens up in a Florida beach condo, watching the digits roll over as beautifully as the surf. I remember sitting there day after day, thinking, "Why am I not happy?"

When I became a financial advisor, I found a way to create meaning through my work: *I would help people create a simple and flourishing life.* At the same time, I vowed to live a simple and flourishing life myself.

In the decade since, I have found a similar pattern repeated in client after client. Whenever a client said they worked only for the sake of making money, at some point they also told me that the work itself had become unsatisfactory and that their overall well-being was suffering regardless of their fiscal success.

Again and again, I have seen my clients become much happier when their business falls into congruence with their beliefs and when they can clearly see the higher purpose it serves.

Unfortunately, busy entrepreneurs often find themselves focused entirely on revenue, market goals, money, and profitability, especially in the beginning years of their businesses. Each of these elements must, of course, be pursued, but not at the expense of the bigger picture.

BEYOND YOUR COMFORT ZONE TO JOY

As humans, we want more than contentment in our happiness; we want actual joy. To get to that level, we must go beyond our comfort zones to seek out moments of total involvement, or what has become known as "flow."

In his influential book *Flow*, Mihaly Csikszentmihalyi argues that as humans, we should always set our goals slightly beyond our reach, and in striving toward those goals, we can achieve the joy of flow.[15]

The goals must not be way beyond our reach but slightly beyond. Unless you are a young and extraordinary athlete, if you set your goal as playing basketball on the same court as an NBA superstar, the result will likely be desperation

---

15   Mihaly Csikszentmihalyi, *Flow: The Psychology of Optimal Experience*, (New York: Harper Perennial Modern Classics, 2008).

and hopelessness. But if you decide to become not just a player but the top scorer in your neighborhood pickup game, you may well experience the deep joy of flow and an optimal experience of total involvement in the game.

English is not my first language, and it's still not the easiest for me. But some years ago, I decided to overcome my fears and tell a personal story in front of an audience at Story District, a Washington, DC-based storytelling show. I was terrified. Indeed, after the first few lines, I felt my carefully rehearsed story was evaporating into thin air. Then, to my amazement, the audience laughed heartily. I got a jolt of adrenaline, I found myself delivering my tale flawlessly, and the emotional high lasted for weeks.

After that, I had one amazing flow experience after another—but only by pushing myself. After I was comfortable doing storytelling, I set the goal of actually doing stand-up comedy and improv in clubs. Now I was moving pretty far outside even my new comfort zone, because in improv, I didn't have time to prepare every word, and the audience was more demanding. The flow, however, only grew stronger.

THE FOUR PILLARS OF WELL-BEING

Now that we understand happiness a little better, let's look at the bigger picture of well-being as part of managing your overall personal "wealth."

Over the years, I have developed what I call my four pillars of well-being. They are very simple: (1) personal growth, (2) business growth, (3) relationships to loved ones, and (4) giving back to community. Underlying these pillars, of course, is the foundation of health.

People talk a lot about finding a "work-life balance," but I do not like that term because it implies that work is somehow not a part of life. I think my four pillars are a much better way of thinking about how to distribute your time and energy.

Each pillar carries *meaning and purpose* as a component of the whole structure, and each should be both *a result and a cause of your happiness.*

1. PERSONAL GROWTH

I do not consider personal growth as a "nice to have" for the entrepreneur. Indeed, I think your personal growth is directly related to your business growth. And of course, as an entrepreneur myself, I know that if your business is not growing, you will be unhappy for sure.

Personal growth means that as a person, you are becoming

more mature, acquiring new skills, expanding your horizons, and broadening your abilities.

I actively attempt to achieve some personal growth every year. For example, I know I grow every time I go to San Francisco, take a musical improv class, and then perform. Who would have thought that someone from China could go on stage, make up English songs, perform reasonably well for an audience, and receive applause? I am keenly aware that my improv and storytelling have not just improved my English but directly worked to improve my rapport with clients and my ability to present my ideas in a compelling and comfortable way.

That is huge for me. What would be huge for you?

2. BUSINESS GROWTH

The next pillar is business growth, which explains itself.

Like you, perhaps, I started my own business from scratch. My language skills were still wanting. Over time, however, I've grown my business enormously. That growth and the effort to overcome many obstacles required a great deal of creativity on my part, as well as initiative, perseverance, persistence, and consistency. All these traits exercised together have resulted in enormous satisfaction, not to mention provided abundantly for my family and me.

Once again, I do not like the term "work-life balance." The growth of my business is not separate from my life it is an enhancement to my life. But if you're reading this book, you probably understand this pillar well and have probably built it strongly. That means you can take some effort to address the other three.

3. RELATIONSHIPS TO LOVED ONES

The next pillar of well-being is formed by the relationships you have with your core family members, including your spouse, children, parents, siblings, and extended relations. I need not explain how important these relationships are in shaping one's happiness and providing meaning to one's efforts.

If I don't have a good relationship at home, it doesn't matter how well my business runs. I won't be very happy, and my well-being will suffer.

Relationships always require mental energy and genuine effort. You will find no shortcuts or ways to delegate this effort. I am a busy man, but I always stop my work when my kids want to play Horse. We also play improv games.

I never fail to find time to put them to sleep, telling them bedtime stories like the Chinese weavers story my grandma told me. I also set specific times aside for my parents, taking them for doctor visits and shopping trips, even though I dislike both waiting rooms and supermarkets.

No one can substitute for me in these endeavors. No one.

4. GIVING BACK TO COMMUNITY

The final pillar of well-being involves your effort to give back to your community, and surely this provides the highest order of happiness.

Martin Seligman's books teach that whatever we do to achieve the highest level of well-being, it must be meaningful and purposeful; however, at some point, that purpose must go above and beyond ourselves. Business and career goals, and even relationships with loved ones, ultimately focus on ourselves. Giving back to the community offers a clearly higher purpose without any direct personal benefit. Without this highest level of meaning, we miss a vital piece of our lives.

For many, the opportunity to give back comes during retirement.

I know an entrepreneur who successfully sold his business

and retired very comfortably in his early sixties. Then an opportunity arose, and he moved himself and his wife to Africa to start a business providing low-cost seeds to farmers in Kenya. Life in northern Virginia was much more comfortable than in the countryside of Kenya, but they sacrificed those comforts in favor of something more meaningful.

Indeed, this couple has found meaning on two levels. One, they are elevating many farmers out of poverty. Second, this man and his wife are devout Christians, and they also see their work as part of their evangelical drive. They live a harder life, but are they happier? Yes, because despite the difficulties, they ultimately have a *higher level of overall well-being* in Africa. They are doing something consistent with their belief as opposed to what they called "wasting time" in northern Virginia.

Another client, who hails from Iran, told me of the many Iranian girls in the countryside who don't get a good education. In retirement, he and his wife are going to set up a nonprofit to help those girls get proper schooling.

Bill Gates devoted the first half of his life building Microsoft and becoming, for many years, literally the wealthiest person on the planet. In those years, he was obsessed with his business, and at the zenith of Microsoft, people often criticized Gates for not giving to charity. During those years, he was actually famous for his lack of philanthropy.

In the second half of his life, however, Gates has devoted himself to giving away his money. He has focused on eradicating diseases, particularly in Africa. And he has said many times that this work has a deeper meaning and gives him even more satisfaction than building Microsoft.

We may be seeing something of the same arc in the astoundingly wealthy and once famously cynical Mark Zuckerberg (see the movie *The Social Network*), who seems to be mellowing since his marriage. His horizons seem to be opening up, and he does seem to be seeing more to the world than making money or outdoing his competitors. Along the way, I hope he finds happiness.

You may, at first, find it hard to believe that giving back to the community is not merely charity or an obligation but a vital part of your own well-being. I can only encourage you to try it and find out for yourself.

MENTAL ENERGY

Each pillar of well-being requires mental energy. There's no getting around that basic fact. As an entrepreneur, you know that good things just don't happen unless you give them attention and make them happen. Few people, however, realize that mental energy is not an unlimited resource; rather, it's a severely limited resource that requires careful management.

As mentioned earlier, research has shown that our minds can make only so many good decisions, perhaps ten, in one day. After that, our abilities decline as our minds become exhausted. This means you absolutely must not waste your thoughts fretting about small things. Again, consider Zuckerberg, who always wears the same gray T-shirt. He has a closet full of them. Why? Because that way, he does not need to waste a moment deciding what to put on each morning. He reserves his mental energy for bigger things.

You may not be a billionaire like Zuckerberg, but as an entrepreneur, you are easily required to make ten important decisions a day. This makes delegation crucial to your overall fund of mental energy. After you delegate a task, you liberate your mind for other purposes, and you preserve that mental fund.

A client of mine who has a mortgage business put it succinctly:

> *If you don't delegate, you don't have a business. All you have is a job.*

I will add this corollary:

> *You will never be able to sell that job to someone else and have them believe it is a business.*

MY LESSON IN DELEGATION

My own natural tendency is to do everything myself.

For years, I ran first my hedge fund and then my financial advisory entirely alone. I hired my first employee only about six years ago—thanks to a video I watched about a successful business owner. In the video, this man said that his goal was to go to his office each day and see nothing on his desk. He saw his job as simply talking to his managers and employees to make sure everything was running properly, then going to play golf.

Unlike this man, I wasn't interested in spending lots of time on the golf course, but the clean desk in the video struck a chord. I realized that I had been hesitant to delegate because I was sure my employees wouldn't do as good a job as I would. If I didn't get over that fear, I'd be overworked forever.

So I bit the bullet and hired an assistant.

At first, I worked just as hard because I didn't trust my assistant with anything important. Only slowly did I realize that if my new employee never got the chance to practice, he would never get to my level of performance, and I would never have a moment's rest. It dawned on me that *I had to allow him to make mistakes and grow in the process.*

It worked. After years together, I now trust him and others with a great deal of crucial work. I just keep two or three functions that are crucial to my business for myself, and I enjoy those. But I now delegate every other function to my assistants. That has liberated so much of my time so that I can have far more life beyond my work. The quality of service to my clients has also increased because I'm not overwhelmed with mundane tasks.

The lesson, especially for lifestyle entrepreneurs like me? Every new hire will indeed cost you time—perhaps an hour a day at first. Indeed, each new employee may take several hours to accomplish what it takes you just fifteen minutes to accomplish. But trust me, it's exciting when you get to the point where they save you that fifteen minutes! Be patient, and they will eventually save you hours and then days, weeks, and years.

THE HIDDEN POWER OF HABIT

Habit is the underlying secret to maintaining all four pillars of your well-being. It's the underlying secret to good health. And beyond the need to delegate, it is certainly the underlying secret to managing your store of mental energy.

If you have the habit of walking a mile each morning before work, you do not have to think about it; you *just do it.* Hence, you have done yourself good without expending any mental energy at all. Indeed, during that walk, you may well add to your store of this precious resource. The same is true of maintaining your family relationships, your business, your charitable work, and all the other components of your well-being.

Habit is not as simple a beast as you may first imagine. I learned about its deeper structure through a book called *The Power of Habit* by Charles Duhigg.[16]

---

16 Charles Duhigg, *The Power of Habit: Why We Do What We Do in Life and Business* (New York: Random House, 2014)

According to Duhigg, habit involves a *trigger*, a *routine*, and then a *reward*. After the trigger is present, we will do the routine, and then we receive the reward. At that point, it becomes a nearly mindless activity for us. This is true of both good and bad habits.

Bad habits are not difficult to analyze and require no therapists to understand. You might, for example, feel isolated and depressed, and this *trigger* causes you to overeat as your *routine*. The *reward* is a jolt of endorphins. Then the cycle repeats. As you become obese, you may become more isolated or depressed. This triggers the same routine and gives you the brief comfort of more food. Result: being overweight and unhappy.

Many of us are also addicted to electronics. A sense of boredom or lack of purpose sends us, by habit, to our email or social media. We get our brief reward of learning some useless fact or watching some silly video. Result: inaction, time wasted, unhappiness.

Thousands of books have been written on how to escape overeating and mild addictions such as electronics. But the secret to overcoming them is ultimately quite simple: *establish a good habit to replace the bad habit and a good reward to replace the bad reward.* When you've established a good habit, you will mindlessly do the right thing for yourself and get a better reward, too.

I have slowly changed my habits for the better by addressing my own personal triggers with the goal of triggering good habits instead of bad. For example, I realized that when I first got up in the morning (the trigger), I used to run to my computer and open my emails. To improve this situation, I placed a yoga mat right in front of my computer. Now, to get to my computer, I have to do twenty minutes of yoga!

The same analysis can be run for the other triggers in your life, whether they be physical triggers (stepping through the door coming home!), time triggers (lunch time!), or emotional triggers (depressed!). Associate a new good habit with the trigger, recognize the reward, repeat the cycle twenty times, and bingo, your life improves.

Always, the key is eliminating choice. If you don't think about your choices or worry about them, you'll just start doing what's best by habit. The rewards may be delayed but will inevitably follow.

AN EXAMPLE OF HABITS IN ALL FOUR PILLARS

As my personal discipline, I have developed habit for all

four pillars. Such routines do not take away from my happiness; they *allow* for my happiness.

To ensure my personal growth, I produce a story show every month, and I produce a musical improv show every quarter. Just like clockwork.

Following the advice of the book *Flow*, I also have a habit of combating the voice in my head that tells me I can't do something. When I see a good stand-up comedy routine and the little voice in my head says, "You're never going to do this," I fight that by saying, "I'm going to do it." Then I take a class so I can perform onstage as well. In this way, I have formed a habit of challenging myself.

In business, I pursue excellent client service by following strict routines. I meet with my clients every three months without fail. Whenever I have a task I think I can delegate, I delegate.

To maintain my relationship with my kids, I still put them to bed and tell them a story every single night, and the story is often improvised. It's sacred daddy and kids time, which requires no planning. Saturday morning is my no-business time. I don't do anything but spend time with the family, going to a museum or a play. I don't have to wonder whether I am going to do this each Saturday, and neither do my kids.

To give back to my community, I try to ensure that charity becomes equally routine. When my second son was born, he had a nasal cleft in his nose, a common deformity. This made me feel for other parents who have kids with facial deformities but no money to fix them. As a result, I donate to a charity called Smile Train. I don't want to think about it every year, so I committed to donate to them for the rest of my life. I set up automatic monthly donations, and I don't plan to ever stop them.

What better use for automation?

You, too, can develop inviolable, decisionless routines around all the four pillars of well-being. Your effort in this area will ultimately prove more important than building your business to some arbitrary size and certainly more important than buying an X45.

Remember the words of Aristotle, surely one of the smartest humans who ever walked the earth:

> *A man is defined not by his extraordinary accomplishments but by his habits.*

Conclusion

What do I hope you remember from this book? My fondest wish is that you should reread it from time to time in order to make sure you remember all six pillars of wealth management and all four pillars of personal well-being and to ensure that you have not forgotten the basic principles of happiness along the entrepreneurial road.

But I will be content with just two big takeaways.

First, I hope you remember that *building and preserving wealth is not the same as building and operating a business.* You must always consider these two activities as completely separate and treat them with different strategies.

Second, I hope that I have convinced you that *just because you are an expert at managing your business doesn't mean you're an expert in managing your wealth.* I hope you now realize that your impressive instincts toward action will likely handicap you as an investor and a money manager, largely because you are just not the kind of person who can sit and watch the grass grow.

Indeed, my greatest fear is that I may still not have convinced you to delegate *any* of the vital tasks needed to build the six pillars of your financial home. After all, in order to build your business in the first place, you had to believe that you were better at building things than anyone you met. Now that you have been armed with knowledge of so many new issues, I fear you may feel even more strongly that you can do this yourself!

So let me present one more argument.

THE CFO ARGUMENT

At some point, if your business grew big enough, you probably hired, or at least considered hiring, a CFO. Even if you were a financial whiz yourself. Even if you had both an MBA degree and a CPA certificate framed in your corner office.

Why? Because you simply didn't have time to do the financial stuff yourself. Even if you knew how. The same is true of your personal finances. Even if you understand all about estate planning, tax mitigation, investment, and more, you simply don't have time to do those things well.

Without an effective delegation strategy for your personal finances, your efforts will always be spread too thin, mistakes will always be made, and one of the six pillars of your financial house will always be neglected. You will also not have time to focus on your overall well-being as a person, which is the one thing you cannot ask anyone else to cover for you.

At some point, to grow your business, you had to delegate some things. At some point, to build your personal life, you have to delegate even more.

START NOW

Entrepreneurs probably have less of a problem with procrastination than any other kind of person I know—except when it comes to their personal finances. When it comes to their own money matters, they seem just as prone to delay as regular humans.

I hope that the minute you turn the last page of this book, you will immediately seek out a qualified, fee-only financial advisor, not just for that overdue review of your tax and investment situation but so you can develop a long-term relationship and use a disciplined, repeatable process.

As a businessperson, you know that mere intention is never enough. It's never enough to say, "I'm really going to give an independent financial advisor a call at some point." You must actually call, email, schedule a meeting, or at least put a firm date on your calendar for when you will do any of the above. After you begin the process, your efforts will gain momentum, and bit by bit, you will build a strong financial house.

You can start by looking at the website of the National Association of Personal Financial Advisors at NAPFA.com. There, you can search for fee-only advisors in your local area.

If you like, you can even engage with me personally through my website, MZCap.com, or email me personally at mzhuang@mzcap.com. I will be happy to reply. At the very least, I could offer you a second opinion financial review.

After that, you must, of course, do your due diligence, conduct your formal interview, and carefully gauge both trust and chemistry. Take this book with you to the meeting and conduct your interview right out of chapter 4.

Take the first step, and you are halfway there.

STEPPING OUT FROM UNDER THE SWORD

I began this book with a story about my friend Damocles, sitting on a throne and looking up to see the sword suspended above his head. That sword was held by a single thread, and as we have learned, similar swords hang over every successful person.

That friend did not get up off his throne in time. As a result, a good man who had devoted his entire life to hard work found himself nearly destitute as he grew older. He had ensured the success of his business but neglected his own well-being and ultimately the well-being of those he loved.

Since that day, I have worked with many other entrepreneurs and seen up close the personal hurdles that come with one of the most demanding jobs on earth. It has been my privilege to help my clients overcome those hurdles, and I hope this book has furthered that work. Perhaps you have found it useful in understanding not just your finances but also your larger challenges and opportunities as a person.

May you build your business to ever greater success.

May you also build your wealth beyond business, and your life beyond work.

END

About the Author

MICHAEL ZHUANG is founder and principal of MZ Capital Management, a wealth advisory with a wide range of successful entrepreneurial clients. He holds dual masters degrees in mathematics and quantitative finance from Carnegie Mellon University. His career in investing included working with Société Général and PG&E, and for the past several years, he has focused on wealth management. He is the author of *Physician Wealth Management Made Easy* and has been a regular contributor to Morningstar and other sites and publications. Michael blogs at the *Investment Fiduciary* and actively pursues his hobby as a stand-up comedian and storyteller.